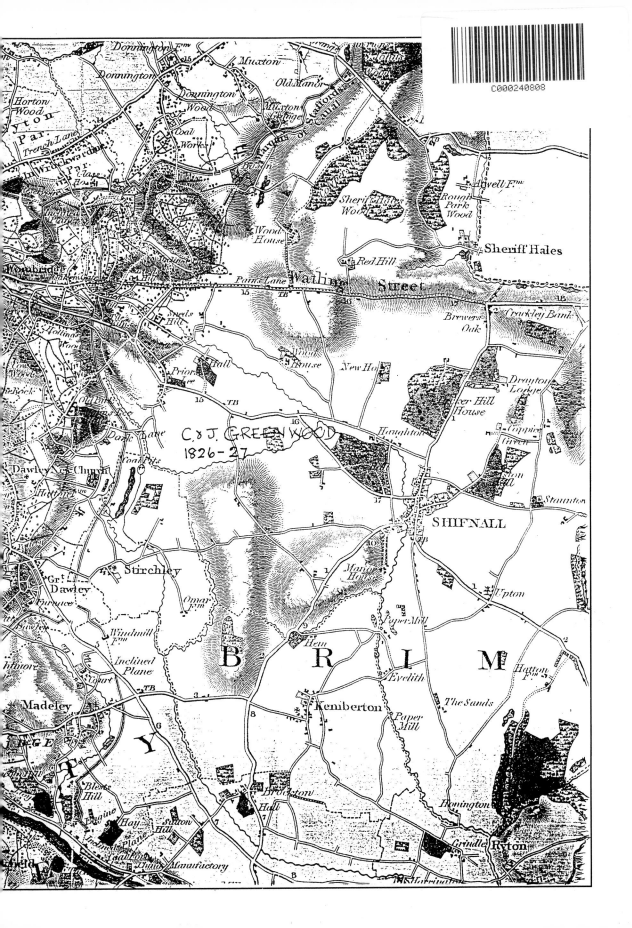

C. & J. GREENWOOD
1826-27

TELFORD
A Pictorial History

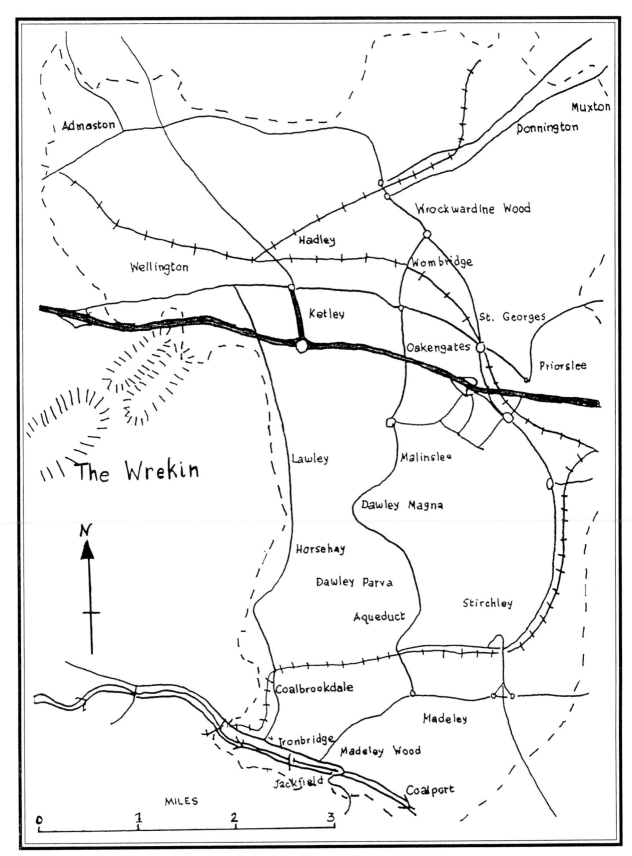

The 'Lost Villages' of Telford

TELFORD
A Pictorial History

To: Joan with best wishes and many thanks.

George Evans
and
Ron Briscoe

George Evans.

Ron Briscoe.

Phillimore

1995

Published by
PHILLIMORE & CO. LTD.,
Shopwyke Manor Barn, Chichester, West Sussex

ISBN 0 85033 955 3

Printed and bound in Great Britain by
BIDDLES LTD.
Guildford, Surrey

We wish to dedicate this book, in true Wellington tradition, to
All Friends round The Wrekin

List of Illustrations

Frontispiece: 'Lost Villages' of Telford

1. Map of Wellington, 1928
2-3. Wellington's Market Square
4. 16th-century building in 1921
5. The *Wrekin Hotel*, the Square
6. Market Square, looking south
7. Victory Parade, 1945
8. Church Street (Market Square)
9. Three shops in the 1920s
10. Advertisement for Richards'
11. New Street, *c.*1920
12. Advertisement for Espley's
13. Heath's, New Street
14. Advertisement for Bates & Hunt
15. L. & D. Morgan, New Street, 1921
16. Cooper Edmonds, photographer
17. Walter Davies, outfitter
18. Tom Grainger's shop
19. S. Corbett & Son, saddler
20. Wesleyan Methodist church
21. Harvey's, Market Street, jewellers
22. Advertisement for Harvey's
23. The Wellington Gas Company, Market Street
24. Declaration of election results, 1906
25. Advertisement for Edward Turner, seed merchant
26. Wrekin Mineral Water Works, Market Street
27. The old Barclays Bank
28. All Saints' Church and Lych Gate
29. St Patrick's Catholic Church, Mill Bank
30. Old Baptist church, King Street
31. Hiatt's Ladies' College
32. Public Library, Walker Street
33. 1930s 'Cook by Electric' advertisement
34. Wellington Cottage Hospital, Haygate Road
35. Tank at Bowring Recreation Ground
36. Christ Church in 1904
37. The *Cock Hotel* and the *Swan*
38. Wellington Town F.C. *Buck's Head*
39. Church Street, looking west
40. Old Hall School, Wellington
41. Class at Old Hall
42. Old Hall Farm
43. Wellington Railway Station
44. Watling Street, Wellington, looking west
45. 'Double Star' jazz band, 1936-7
46. 'Good Night Vienna' Clifton Cinema, 1939
47. Coronation of King George V, 1911
48. Coronation crowd, Market Street, 1911
49. Wrekin College
50. Wrekin College rugby team
51. Wellington & District Cottage Hospital
52. Primitive Methodist church, Tan Bank
53. Mill Bank, Wellington
54. Map of Hadley, 1928
55. Watery Lane, Hadley
56. Hadley Council School
57. Hadley Park windmill
58. Advertisement for Blockleys Ltd.
59. Guillotine lock on Union Canal
60. Hadley Park Farm
61. Joseph Sankey's works, 1918
62. Hadley Orpheus Male Voice Choir, 1925
63-4. Apley Castle
65. Map of Ketley, 1928
66. Ketley Station, *c.*1900
67. Priorslee Furnaces
68. John Maddock & Co., Oakengates
69. Oakengates town band, 1930
70. Molineux, butchers, 1913
71. Corfield's, grocer's, 1918
72. Old ambulance, 1930
73. New ambulance, 1938
74. Oakengates Wakes, 1905
75. Bridge Street, Oakengates, 1935
76. Snedshill Brickworks, 1940
77. Scout troop, Oakengates, 1919
78. View from Albion Pit Bank, 1928
79. Corfields and cart, 1920
80. Oakengates Green and market, 1925
81. Grosvenor Cinema in the 1920s
82. Holyhead Road, Oakengates, 1905
83. Staff at Wombridge school
84. Snedshill Forge
85. View of Oakengates
86-7. Oakengates railway tunnel
88. The *Royal Exchange*, Oxford Street
89. Oakengates
90. Oakengates Green and the Coffee Palace
91. The Oakengates Park
92. Wombridge church
93. Holy Trinity Church
94. John Maddock & Co. Ltd.
95. Wrockwardine Wood Methodist church
96. St Georges Institute
97. Great foundry and factory, Lilleshall Co.
98. St Georges Methodist church

99. St George's Church
100. Boot scraper
101. Temperance band, 1905
102. William Shuker with Sir John Barbirolli
103. Market Street, Oakengates
104. Wrekin ales, beer and mineral waters
105. Priorslee Hall Gardens
106. The library, Priorslee Hall
107. Priorslee Furnaces
108. Priorslee coal distillation plant
109. Map of Oakengates, St Georges and Priorslee
110. Map of Dawley, 1928
111. High Street, Dawley, in the 1920s
112. *Queen's Head Inn*, The Finger
113. The 'Pig on the Wall' postcard
114. St Leonard's Church, Malinslee
115. Malinslee railway station
116. Ruins of Norman chapel
117-8. The lights and fountain monument to Matthew Webb
119. St Luke's Church, Doseley
120. Langley School, Dawley
121. Dark Lane fields
122. Dark Lane, The Rows
123. Horsehay Pool
124. Station Road, Horsehay
125. Horsehay Works
126. The Round House, Horsehay
127. Horsehay Works
128. Shed being erected at Horsehay
129. Cottages in Queen Street, Madeley
130. Park Street, Madeley
131. St Michael's Church
132. Wesleyan chapel
133. The Madeley Methodist church
134. Anstice Memorial Hall
135. View from St Michael's Church tower
136. Coke Hearth, Lightmoor

137. Jiggers Bank in the 19th century
138. Looking west from Jiggers Bank
139. Map of Ironbridge and Coalbrookdale in 1902
140. Coalbrookdale from the south
141. Lumhole waterfall
142. Holy Trinity Church
143. Coalbrookdale from Bentall Edge
144-5. The Rotunda, Coalbrookdale
146. Coalbrookdale railway station
147. Rose Cottage
148. Coalbrookdale County High School
149. The Bridge
150. Ironbridge, a print of 1850
151-2. The Wharfage, Ironbridge
153. Ironbridge from the south
154. Ironbridge railway station, *c*.1907
155. St Luke's Church
156. Albert Edward Bridge
157. Benthall Edge ferry
158. Passage-boat, Jackfield
159. Great Water Wheel
160. The Coalport and Jackfield Memorial Bridge
161. St Mary's Church at Jackfield
162. Tommy Rogers, with coracle
163. Free Bridge, Coalport
164. Coalport incline and basin
165. China Works, Coalport
166. Bottle Kiln, 1968
167. Coalport Bridge
168. The ironworks, Blisses (Blists) Hill
169. The Wrekin from the Ercall
170. The Wrekin from Cressage
171. Artesian Well
172. The Ercall from the Wrekin
173. The Forest Glen Pavilion
174. Wrekin Upper Cottage (Halfway House)
175. The Needle's Eye, The Wrekin

Acknowledgements

George Evans and Ron Briscoe would like to express their gratitude for the help of many of their friends in compiling this book. In particular the following have contributed illustrations: Councillor Philip Morris-Jones, 11, 24, 27, 28, 30, 31, 34, 37, 40-3, 49, 50, 111, 112, 117, 123-5, 129, 130, 139-48, 154-9, 161, 164, 166, 168, 170, 173, 175; Mrs. Rae Green of the Commission for New Towns, 2, 57-61, 69-90, 93-102, 105-8, 115, 116, 118-22, 126-8, 131, 132, 134-7, 149-53, 160, 162, 163, 165, 167, 169; Mr. Fred Brown, 4, 7, 9, 13-16, 18, 23, 26, 29, 35, 36, 45, 47, 48, 54-7, 62, 65, 66, 100, 104, 113, 174; Mrs. Margery Johnson, 10, 12, 14, 22, 25, 33, 58, 46, 162; Mr. Barry Felton, 3, 5, 6, 8, 17, 19-21, 32, 38, 39, 44, 51-3, 63, 64, 67, 91, 92, 103, 114, 133, 171, 172.

We are also most grateful to Mrs. Naomi Evans, who has given many, many hours to proof reading and advising. Her support and encouragement have been essential.

Introduction

Although a new town created in the 1960s, Telford has within its boundaries a remarkable range of histories. The new development was built in the spaces between much older settlements. Some of these were already ancient when Domesday Book was written; others achieved fame in the early 18th century as the world's most advanced industrial area. Telford is only the latest of a series of events in the long history of this quite unique place.

Until 1968 there was no town called Telford. In many ways there still is not, for within its boundaries there are in fact several towns and villages. There is no local government unit named Telford; it is a designated area within the district of The Wrekin containing the parishes of Wellington, Hadley, Ketley, Lawley, Oakengates, Priorslee and St Georges, Greater Dawley, Dawley Hamlets, Madeley and The Gorge, together with parts of other parishes. This is not a place where everything was obliterated to clear space for new development; the new had to be fitted between the old.

So *Telford: A Pictorial History* is not the short story of a new town but an account of an area whose activities have spanned many centuries. The World Heritage Site of the Ironbridge Gorge Museum exhibits some of the most fascinating aspects of the past, but it must be remembered that many of Telford's communities were active a thousand years before the great iron bridge was built.

Perhaps the first exciting event happened soon after the melting of the ice at the end of the last Ice Age, when a huge lake overflowed, changing the course of the river Severn and gouging out the steep sided Ironbridge Gorge. This relatively recent happening (in geological terms) is still settling down and there are minor landslips from time to time.

Geologically much more ancient are the pre-Cambrian rocks of The Wrekin, thrust up by a series of faults which were active for several millions of years. The East Shropshire coalfield, source of much of the area's power and raw materials, is also heavily faulted. Most of Telford is within this coalfield, though some of the Weald Moors to the north and Wellington and Admaston in the west are included.

The Carboniferous rocks provided not only coal but also iron ore, limestone for flux, and clay for building. Streams powered the water wheels. The Severn became a highway. But before the 18th century any wealth there was here was earned from the land by farming and forestry. Only in later centuries have the minerals been more important than the soil above them. Now the raw materials are exhausted, and wealth is produced by the skills of the people.

Tax values reported in Domesday were in every case lower than they had been before 1086. In each instance of manors within the Telford designated area the values had increased by the 13th century. Market charters were issued to most Shropshire towns, for example Wellington's right to an earlier market was confirmed by a charter of 1244. At this time the once great forest of The Wrekin, or Mount Gilbert as it had been called for a time, was being rapidly cleared. Much of this area belonged to the Church; to the monasteries of Wenlock, Buildwas, Haughmond, Lilleshall and Wombridge. There was iron-making, bell-casting, leather-making and especially the cloth trade, mostly centred on Wellington which had recently supplanted Wrockwardine as the administrative centre of the hundred.

After the dissolution of the monasteries Lilleshall's land was bought by a Wolverhampton merchant from whom are descended the Levesons and Leveson Gowers, who became lords of Gower, earls of Stafford and dukes of Sutherland. More importantly, they founded the Lilleshall Company which drained the Weald Moors and developed canals, railways, mines, foundries, engineering factories and brickworks in Oakengates, Wrockwardine Wood and St Georges.

The Civil War can be said to have started in Wellington, for King Charles mustered his troops at Orleton Park and made a great speech which was virtually a declaration of war against his parliament: 'Gentlemen, you have heard these orders read; it is your part, in your several places, to observe them exactly. The time cannot be long before we come to action ...'. There were no major battles here, only minor skirmishes, but troops of both sides, living off the country, impoverished the inhabitants. The war caused much devastation; Apley Castle and Wellington church were left in ruins while Dawley Castle, which had resisted the Round-heads, was destroyed.

In 1709 Abraham Darby revolutionised the world's ironfounding trade by using coke to fire his furnaces instead of the charcoal which had supplied fuel for the previous 2,000 years. By providing cheaper and better iron he enabled many new inventions to be developed, triggering the movement later called the Industrial Revolution. He and his successors, Abraham Darby II, III and IV, enabled this area to become the leading industrial district in the world.

Other notable figures included John Wilkinson (nicknamed 'Iron Mad' because of his obsession for making everything from iron), Richard Trevithick (who invented the steam engine), John Rose (the developer of fine china at Coalport) and William and Richard Reynolds (relatives of the Darbys and co-founders of the Coalbrookdale Company). Not to be forgotten, however, are the many working men and women whose skills and labour made fame and fortune for their masters.

In the north of the area the Lilleshall Company developed into a huge trading complex from its founding in the middle of the 18th century. It competed with the Coalbrookdale Company to the south. Both were involved in inventions of iron rails, bridges, aqueducts, window frames, engines and the many other exciting new products.

Tub boat canals came early and, with locks and inclined planes, became the main means of carrying goods to the chief trading artery, the river Severn. Thomas Telford came briefly past, designing Madeley church, some of the canals and rebuilding the road from London to Holyhead. With the introduction of railways in the 19th century the axis of trade moved from the Severn north to the Wellington-Oakengates line, augmented by a complex system of minor lines, works sidings and narrow gauge tracks. Another reason for the shift was that much of the coal and iron to the south was exhausted and the deeper seams to the east were being worked by new mining technology. The Roman Watling Street became the A5 as roads became more important, eventually being superseded by the M54 motorway. Railways seem destined to join canals in history.

With the large increase of population the churches in some places were finding it diffi-cult to cope. Most of the landowners were Anglican but the Darby family and others were Quakers. Baptists and Congregationalists increased in number and at times enlarged their churches. Many Roman Catholics arrived, mainly from Ireland. John Fletcher of Madeley, friend and biographer of John Wesley, encouraged Methodism and there were many chapels of both Wesleyan and Primitive Methodists, often associated with charismatic preachers. The churches and chapels led campaigns against cock-fighting, gambling and excessive drinking. In spite of the steady decline in church attendance this century the variety has increased, and now includes eastern Orthodox, West Indian Adventist and Pentecostal churches, a Sikh temple, Muslim Mosque and many Hindus.

The invention of photography at the end of the 19th century resulted in many picture postcards being produced of the area, both by national firms and local publishers. Most depicted scenes which people would like to send to their friends and relations, such as The Wrekin, Wellington Market Square and the Iron Bridge, but some are more interesting than beautiful. These are now much collected, especially by members of the Telford Philatelic Society. Book publishing, after an early start and decline, has enjoyed a rebirth. A list of some recommended reading is included in the bibliography at the end of this book.

Local newspapers began halfway through the last century and continue to prosper. For over fifty years the *Wellington Journal and Shrewsbury News* dominated the market in Shropshire and neighbouring counties. Now this is reduced to *The Telford Journal*, a 'freebie', whose news sections are greatly reduced, though within its restrictions its efforts are heroic. The main local paper is now *The Shropshire Star*, which outsells all national papers in Shropshire.

By the 20th century the economy had changed from farming and forestry to manufacture, though until the coming of Telford there was still agriculture between the industrial towns and villages. Fortunes soared at first but later slumped; this happened several times as trade changed and new factories took the place of outdated technology or moved to other places. On occasion there was destitution and emigration; at other times workers were attracted from far afield. Some places were prosperous while others were in dire need. This is still the case after 25 years of massive intervention and draconian planning powers.

Because of the great variety of ways in which individual settlements in this area have developed their unique histories and personalities it is thought best, after this very brief survey of the whole district, to look more closely at the towns and villages which still make up the bulk of the population. The order of both this account and the illustrations is as we would read a book—from north-west to south-east.

Wellington, Wrockwardine and **Admaston** are on the north-western edge of Telford. At Domesday they were in the Wrockwardine hundred—the village had been founded as the headquarters of the Wreoken Saetan who ruled the former Romano-Celtic lands of the Cornovii. However fortunes changed and by 1244 Wellington had acquired a market charter and was developed as a market town, whilst Wrockwardine remained a farming village. Admaston was to become known as the richest village in Shropshire—the reason was its railway station which made it an affluent dormitory suburb of Wellington. Admaston Spa also contributed to its popularity.

Wellington developed as the chief market for east Shropshire and shared in the profits of the industrial development to the east. There had been cloth-processing industries, leather-making and bell-founding in medieval times. Later the Shropshire works of Richard Groom and Son, timber merchants of Bridge Road, Wellington, became 'the country's largest timber buyers' and many associated trades, such as furniture-making, developed. The Excelsior Carriage Works made carriages 'for the Empire'. Corbett's made agricultural implements, including 'the world's finest grinding mill'; Bromley's and Clay's were also in the same trade. William Edwards developed the coal-gas making and supplied a large area. There was also manufacture of dolls by Chad Valley and Nora Wellings; Addison's made school furniture.

Wellington's passenger railway station was a joint Great Western Railway and London, Midland and Scottish Railway affair and the main junction for the east of the county. There were main lines to Shrewsbury, Wolverhampton, Stafford and Crewe, with branch lines covering the coalfield towns and villages and a link to the Severn Valley Railway, Wenlock and Craven Arms. The goods station handled a variety of freight, especially coal, timber and animals for the Smithfield auction. This enabled the fat-stock market and wool sales to grow into the largest in the West Midlands as it was most convenient for city buyers of London and Birmingham.

Famous Wellington people include Dr. William Withering, a local practitioner and contemporary of Darwin who discovered a market-trader more successful at treating heart disease than himself, bought her medicine (which contained foxgloves), analysed it and became the discoverer of digitalis; he also helped found the anti-slavery society. Another resident was Sarah Smith, born in New Street, who wrote 'improving' stories under the *nom-de-plume* of Hesba Stretton and outsold her mentor, Charles Dickens, publishing 1,500,000 copies of *Jessica's First Prayer*. Sarah Smith helped found the London Children's Society, which became the NSPCC.

Until the arrival of Telford, Wellington was the transport, market, administrative, educational and professional centre for the area. *The Wellington Journal* was the Shropshire weekly paper. This was the second largest market town in the county and drew business from a hinterland with a population of over 60,000. The new town planners' decision to treat it as one of several 'district centres' was not popular.

Hadley may be the oldest place in the area. A bronze palstave was found there, dating from perhaps 1000 B.C. The name, however, is Saxon and it first appears in public, and in Domesday, as one of the hamlets of the parish of Wellington. Although it has had its own parish for a century, Hadley tends to look to Wellington as its market town. It is very much a place of industry, especially of steel pressings at GKN Sankey, formerly Joseph Sankey and Son. Here was Europe's largest manufacturer of wheels, chassis and steel furniture, where during the Second World War Spitfires were made, and more recently armoured personnel vehicles. Here also are Blockley's who make bricks and paviors from local clay, producing, incidentally, several delightful wildlife pools from the holes where clay was extracted. Another large industry was wire-making at Haybridge Steel Works. Hadley also has a varied cultural life, with fine choirs at both Anglican and Methodist churches, a lively West Indian centre with a steel band, and a Sikh temple. The districts of Leegomery and Apley are in Hadley parish.

Donnington consists mainly of the Base (formerly Central) Ordnance Depot, one of the army's main stores, which moved from Woolwich in 1938-9, together with housing for its workers and barracks for the soldiers. The depot itself comprises several huge sheds, some capable of containing 1,000 office workers; others are storehouses. Walkers of Donnington made steel containers of various sizes, but sadly are no longer there. Many inhabitants are, or are descended, from Londoners moved for safety, but there are also what used to be called DPs (displaced persons) who came to England for asylum during and after the war.

Trench, between Hadley and Donnington, owes its name to the canal which passed this way, and a very early inclined plane by means of which barges were transferred between high and low level canals. There are a variety of industries at Trench and Trench Lock, including Russell Rubber, which makes car components.

Ketley, south of Hadley and east of Wellington, is also an ancient settlement with its own parish and a great deal of industry. As well as Ketley there are Ketley Sands, Ketley Brook, Ketley Bank, Ketley Town and Ketley Dingle. The largest factory was once part of the Darby empire and is still connected with Coalbrookdale. Known as Glynwed (or Sinclair's) it includes a foundry for castings. Across the road is Aga, manufacturer of the famous grates; formerly it made agricultural implements for James Clay. Another Ketley industry is printing the *Shropshire Star*.

Horton and **Hortonwood** are parts of the Weald Moors which were incorporated into Telford. These lands were shallow pools, marsh and bog until they were drained by the Leveson Gower family and their Lilleshall Company. Before Telford this was a most productive farming area due to the high quality of the peat and clay soils. The land is now covered with new factories, many of which are Japanese, German and Korean.

Oakengates used to advertise itself on its railway bridge as 'The brightest little town in Salop'. Although quite ancient it was a small part of Wombridge until the railway station encouraged the development of the shopping centre. There has been a great deal of industry here including Maddocks' iron foundry, and a large complex of the Lilleshall Company at Snedshill which produced steel and bricks. There was once a highly complicated transport system, with a canal, light railway, several roads and two main railway lines—all in the same place, all going in different directions. It makes 'Spaghetti Junction' look simple. Oakengates had a coffee palace until the Development Corporation demolished it. The thriving shopping centre has now been surrounded by a one-way ring road and mainly superseded by Telford's shopping malls. The Roman Watling Street passed through the High Street, but deviated from its usual straight line to climb the hill into St Georges. Before 1974 Oakengates was an urban district, but local parish government was suspended in that year until 1988, when two parishes were created; Oakengates Town and the parish of St Georges and Priorslee.

Wombridge was once the local priory, a few ruins of which are in the churchyard. It has for a long time been part of Oakengates and is now mainly residential. During the time of the priory there was iron-working, using local ore and charcoal and, at one time, the monks were instructed to use less wood. The iron production remained the same. Either they anticipated Darby's invention and used coked coal or by means of 'creative accounting' they continued with charcoal.

St Georges, previously known as Pains Lane, was developed by the Lilleshall Company. It is now mainly a residential area and includes an interesting country park on the site of Shropshire's last coal mine, the 1,000 ft. deep Granville Colliery. There is a cutting on Queensway (A442) illustrating in coloured bricks the seams and faults of the coalfield. East of the town is Red Hill, probably the site of a Roman marching camp called Uxacona. To the north is Muxton, which has several ancient timber-framed houses.

Wrockwardine Wood formerly belonged to Wrockwardine, but now the only wooded parts are old pit mounds like the Cockshutt, which have mainly regenerated naturally into post-industrial habitat, a most fascinating ecological system. There are also old and new industries including a former glass factory which used slag from Donnington Wood furnaces, refractory bricks from Horsehay and basalt from Little Dawley to make crown glass and dark green bottles for the French wine trade.

Priorslee, the clearing belonging to Wombridge Priory, was the site of the headquarters of the Lilleshall Company at Priorslee Hall. This became the offices of Telford Development

Corporation and is now the nucleus of the University in Shropshire, a college of the University of Wolverhampton. There have been many mines in the area and also a steelworks.

Dawley was a forest clearing within The Wrekin Forest, a farming area known to have iron ore and coal below its fields. During the Middle Ages a castle was built which survived until it declared for the king during the Civil War—it was demolished after Parliament had won. The site, like many parts of Dawley, was used for an ironworks and what remains of the castle's stones have lain for many years under a great mound. The most famous Dawley man was Captain Matthew Webb, the first man to swim the English Channel, who lost his life attempting the Niagara whirlpool. The heavy industry on which the town was based fluctuated greatly and has now changed and moved. There were at one time many small 'back garden' mines, often bell pits, which required little equipment to work. The area which is now Dawley's town centre used not to be the middle of the village, but was called Dawley Market; it became the focus of the town as it developed. The High Street, where traffic on the A442 struggled, is now pedestrianised, which allows a lively market to be held in the street and many of the shops have remained in spite of competition from Telford's malls.

Little Dawley or Dawley Parva still has some old houses and fine pools. Domesday credits the village with a villanus, two bordars and a serf, with woodlands probably making up most of the land. In 1871 the population was 2,451; perhaps more than today, with seven farmers, two chartermasters, a haulier, two grocers, a carpenter, blacksmith, butcher, relieving officer, vicar and registrar.

Dawley Bank had been an agricultural area in the early 19th century with some shallow pits, but it developed rapidly with mining and industry. Most of the pits were on the west side of the Lightmoor fault, where coal is near the surface and was easier to get than in the deeper seams of the east. By the latter part of the same century it was in decline and there was an emigration officer; many families went to Australia.

Malinslee has an interesting church which was influenced, if not designed, by Thomas Telford. Malin, after whom this forest clearing was named, was a woman. From the 13th to the 16th century it was part of Leegomery parish and administered from Eyton. Here the Botfields of Old Park and Dark Lane built a huge iron complex with attendant mines, forges, mills and three blast furnaces. Work was begun in 1790 and lasted a century. Improvements in chain-making invented here by Gilbert Gilpin were widely adopted. James Pool of the *Wickets Inn* made boilers and nails, and Old Park also had a brickworks.

Dosely has a black basalt rock which, in places, has a columnar structure like the Giant's Causeway, or the 'dhu' stone of Clee Hill. The rock was used for many industrial purposes and the formation also provided a small tourist attraction. There were bricks made and later salt-glazed pipes. The name Prawn Hatchet near Dosely refers to a gate leading into a wood in medieval times.

Madeley is an ancient town, a forest clearing on the Mad Brook. For a very long time the lords of the manor were the abbots of Wenlock and until 1965 all its lands were in the borough of Wenlock. It was the largest non-metropolitan borough in England for several centuries until reorganisation in 1974. Historically Madeley included Madeley Wood, Coalbrookdale and what later became Ironbridge and Coalport. The parish church of

St Michael was built by Thomas Telford on the site of a pre-Christian burial mound. It is an unusual octagonal shape and its most famous priest was the Swiss John Fletcher, a friend and biographer of John Wesley. The Rev. Fletcher is buried in a cast-iron tomb in the churchyard.

The Court House is a fine building following its renovation and extension prompted by its conversion to an hotel. Here the Brooke family lived, adapting it from a grange of Wenlock Priory which had been bought by Sir Robert Brooke, former speaker of the House of Commons. His descendants leased their furnace at Coalbrookdale to Abraham Darby I, where he developed his method of making cast-iron using coke rather than the charcoal which had been used for many centuries. Thomas Randall of Madeley made fine porcelain and Lord Moulton, reportedly a charming man and a former lawyer at the Court of Appeal, made over a million tons of explosives for the War Office.

An interesting building is Anstice Hall, the first working men's club in England. It has been renovated and now, surrounded by new buildings, it forms the focus of what is left of the shopping area. This is some way from the old centre; when the railway came it caused a new market to be set up, distinguished from the original settlement as Madeley Market. The old vicarage and an ancient barn where King Charles II is reputed to have hidden have both survived new developments.

Horsehay was for many years a great industrial centre. Both the Coalbrookdale Company and its rival John 'Iron Mad' Wilkinson were owners of factories in the area. Earlier industry had a 'ginny rail' or light railway using horses for traction from the Limekiln Woods and Black Hayes to bring limestone and coal to the foundry. Here were made bridges for export all over the world, including the bridge over the Victoria Falls. Later the same works made large cranes, after being the pioneers of 'Sentinel' coal-burning trucks. These machines were great snorting, thundering monsters, which were later built in Shrewsbury, but a change in the law which strictly limited the amount of smoke emission, noise and weight permitted for a vehicle on the public highway killed the trade.

Coalport, south of Madeley, has its own iron bridge, built in 1792, across to the *Woodbridge Inn*, which is presumably older than the bridge. The village is most famous for its fine china works, begun by John Rose and ended when the company moved to The Potteries in 1926, though the name is still used. Coalport was a new town but is now mainly concerned with the Ironbridge Gorge Museum, among whose exhibits are the tar tunnel and inclined plane.

Coalbrookdale, the valley of the Caldebrook, was ideally placed for the development of Abraham Darby's ironworks. Coal, iron and limestone were all readily available and easily moved downhill to the site; water-power to drive the great wheel powering the huge bellows which supplied air was plentiful. Finally the markets were easily reached from the river Severn, which connected with the ports. Skilled workers were also here for this was already an iron-working area. These conditions which contributed to the rise of the industry were also responsible for its fall, for the narrow valley was restrictive and raw materials ran out. Prosperity gave way to decline, and finally to preservation and museum tourism. Here many of the great inventions began: ironworks powered by coke, iron rails, steam engines, iron-framed buildings, iron window-frames, iron coffins and, of course, the great iron bridge.

One of the most prolific inventors was Thomas Parker, whose memorial tablet is in Coalbrookdale church; he was responsible for developing many of the electrical devices in common use, including trams and the London Underground. Now the village still makes castings at the old works, and lower down the valley at Dale End the Merrythought factory produces teddy bears.

Ironbridge was part of Madeley Wood before Abraham Darby III and John Wilkinson employed Thomas Farnolds Pritchard to design the great bridge. The design still evokes wonder and many unanswered questions, such as whether it was influenced by wooden bridges and the great puzzlement of how, exactly, it was assembled in 1779, with boats and ships constantly using the waterway below. The wharfage was once one of the great river ports, with large numbers of Severn trows and other craft landing and taking on their cargoes there. Among the trows were many smaller craft including the coracles which plied across and up and down the stream, survivors from at least Celtic times and used mainly for fishing. Houses spread up the steep and unstable sides of the gorge as the population swelled in response to the prosperity of the factories. Many foundries, including Bedlam furnace, together with ancillary industries which finished the goods and used by-products, mushroomed along the riverside and up the hill. No wonder it was described by Charles Hulbert in 1837 as 'the most extraordinary district in the world'. Exhibits in the Ironbridge Gorge Museum go far to depict the wonder of it all and the hive of activity it became. They cannot, however, reproduce the stench and the sweat, the toil and the fear, the danger and the misery which came with the marvels. Nor can the social conditions be reproduced, the terrible poverty which was experienced by those without work, despite the best efforts of certain employers such as the caring Quaker Darbys. Perhaps this is just as well, for one can hardly imagine the reactions of the thousands of tourists who converge on the World Heritage Site from all over the world if the worst of the past were displayed with the exciting best.

There is so much to be said of Ironbridge's unique place in history and no room for it here. Fortunately several writers, especially Barrie Trinder, have given it much more space than we have; we can only recommend that readers follow up the theme.

The Wrekin is not in Telford but overshadows it all and has dominated events in East Shropshire since long before it was first called Shropshire a mere thousand years ago. Romans and Saxons named their regional capitals after the prominent hill. The suggestion that The Wrekin was the site of worship centuries before Christianity came, is supported by the continuing tradition of Easter worship on the top. There is still a strong local affinity and respect which has been compared with the Japanese treatment of Mount Fuji. The district council, parliamentary seat and many firms, houses and roads are called after The Wrekin. Local people, asked for a name for the new town, said Wrekin, though this was ignored by the minister concerned.

Throughout the 18th and 19th centuries fairs were held on the hilltop each May. Originally they were trade fairs dealing with wool, horses and cattle, but later they became an excuse for celebrating the joys of getting drunk and were discontinued when they developed into drunken brawls between colliers and yeomen. Many people spent their holiday walking from their homes in Oakengates, Dawley, Ironbridge or Madeley to the summit, and then back home again. Once the railways had arrived church and works trips would travel from the Black Country to Wellington by train, then to the Forest Glen by horse or motor charabanc, and once there the ascent would be attempted on foot. The expression to 'go all round The Wrekin', meaning to take a circuitous route or to do something the longest way, is quite common in the West Midlands. The Forest Glen was a refreshment pavilion at the foot of the hill near the route where it is most easily climbed. Set up in 1889 it was operated by the

Pointon family for nearly a century. It has since been demolished and re-erected at the Blists Hill Museum. The building provided refreshment for travellers and also did a lively trade as a venue for dinners and dances in the evenings throughout the year, always including the famous toast to 'All Friends Round The Wrekin', used all over the world when there are gatherings of people from this part of the country.

The summit is surrounded by a hillfort, the chief settlement of the people called Cornovii by the Romans, until the new town of Viroconium Cornoviorum (Wroxeter) took its place. A number of rocks were probably used for worship; the Needle's Eye is still climbed with difficulty by the young, as they have done for many centuries. The hill is a hog's back ridge produced by the Caledonian Orogenesis, a mountain building system. Other hills in the range are the Ercall, St Lawrence, Maddocks Hill and Little Hill. Most of the rocks are ancient pre-Cambrian and Cambrian; some are volcanic, though there was never a volcano. Until the 13th century the whole of this area was part of the royal forest of The Wrekin (for a time the forest of Mount Gilbert).

People, however, are the greatest asset of the area now known as Telford. There are a few famous names but such a fascinating variety of ordinary unique individuals; this is the real wealth of 'The most extraordinary district in the world'.

1 This 6": 1 mile Ordnance Survey map of Wellington in 1928 seems at first glance similar to today's town. Differences include the disappearance of the Smithfield, the railway sidings, Groom's timber works, the Gasworks and all three foundries. Now there are more car parks, an inner ring road and many houses to the north and south. The narrow medieval streets in the centre remain.

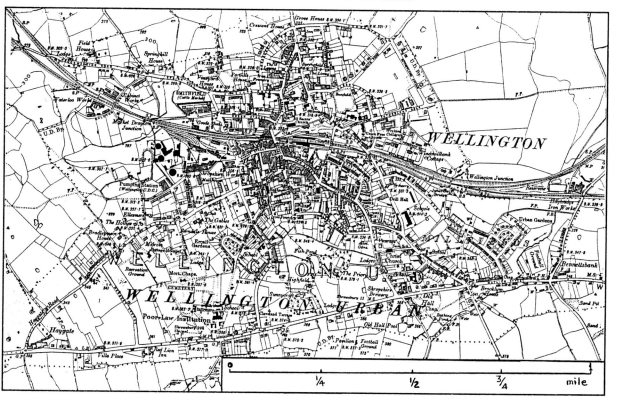

2   Wellington's Market Square has changed little since its Market Charter was granted in 1244, confirming a previous market, probably on the Green. From at least 1680 until around 1800 there was a building here with a court house above, and an open butter market below. The market moved to its present building to the west in 1868 and has since expanded several times.

3   In 1900 the Square was still centre of the town, though the market had already moved to its present location off Market Street. The horse and cart was the typical form of transport and much of the market's farm and garden produced was carried in this way. Railways also moved both people and goods, but cars were still rare.

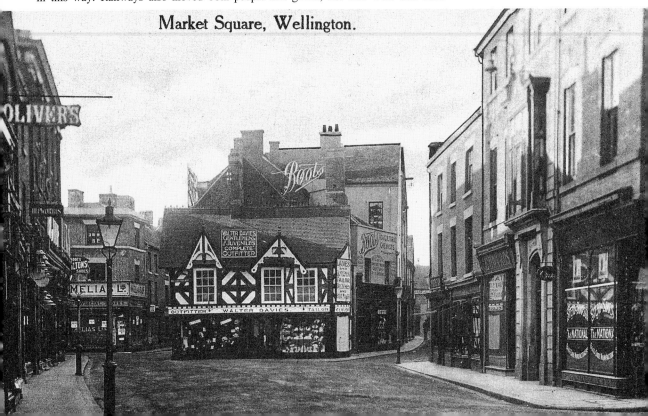

Market Square, Wellington.

4 Walter Davies, above left, was an important outfitters for both men and boys. The shop was situated at 1 The Square and part of the building, which is much smaller than it looks, is 16th-century in origin. In the Victorian period additions to the right-hand side of the building were made and the timber-framing was painted on to make it look much older.

5 The *Wrekin Hotel*, above right, was built on the corner of the Square and Market Street and occupies a dominating position. Originally the hotel included all the ground floor, but by 1920 only the grand entrance remained; now this too has been taken over and is part of a shop. It became a 'commercial hotel', catering for commercial travellers. Mrs. Chinnock, the proprietor, kept a parrot and had a reputation for eccentricity.

6 In the 1930s the Square was beginning to have more multiple shops and less individual 'owner-occupied' premises. This was the scene of a Fascist rally led by Sir Oswald Mosley, which almost turned into a riot leaving Sir Oswald and his Blackshirts bruised, battered, and very lucky to have escaped.

Wellington, Market Square, looking South.

7 In 1945 after V.E. and V.J. Day a parade was held in Market Square—more out of a sense of relief that the war had ended than in celebration. However large numbers of local men and women, including both authors, were still away on active service and were not able to take part in the event.

8 This is not Market Square as stated on the postcard but Church Street; the photographer had his back to the Square. On the right is the parish churchyard and the old post office is in the centre with Lloyds Bank on the left. Next to the bank is a narrow alley called Ten Tree Croft, a corruption of tentercroft, where newly-processed cloth was hung on tenter hooks.

captivating . . .

and exclusive are the correct terms for our New Designs of Linen and Leather Handbags for Spring and Summer Wear.

for Handbags
of style

RICHARDS

Market Square : Wellington

9 The three shops, above left, were demolished in 1973 after almost half a century of service. Children began with Noblett's sweetshop before graduating to Richards' tobacconists, where the tobacco was kept in jars and mixed to the customer's requirements. Brittain's sold cakes downstairs and ran a café on the first floor. John Menzies' new shop replaced all three.

10 Richards', above right, was a ladies' and gentlemen's hairdressers as well as tobacconists so they naturally sold walking sticks, umbrellas and handbags! This advertisement was taken from the programme for an amateur dramatic and musical performance in 1939; Bert Richards was a keen performer.

11 New Street, *c.*1920. On the right is the *Duke of Wellington* (not that the Iron Duke had anything to do with this Wellington). Here was a haven of strict decorum; Alf Langley the proprietor was very particular as to who was allowed in. Drinks were served in cut-glass and swearing was strictly forbidden. Many of the buildings in the foreground have since been demolished.

12 Espley's, left, was the leading pork butchers for many miles around. People would come from near and far to buy their pork pies and sausages. It was said that every part of the pig was used except the squeal! The slaughterhouse was at the back of the shop, entered via Bell Street, previously called Swinemarket.

13 Heath's, below left, baked their own confectionery at the back of the cake shop and had a restaurant above. The quality of their cakes was famous. They also had an 'annexe' in the yard which was let for weddings; this later grew into the Town House. It is a surprise that they also supplied the Forest Glen (see illustration 173).

14 Bates and Hunt, below right, was an old established chemist's. There were two shops in Wellington—this shop in New Street being a listed building. The many wonderful jars labelled 'leeches' and other exotic remedies are now in a reconstruction at Blists Hill Museum. They also sold Zambuk, Carters' Liver Pills and California Syrup of Figs.

15 L. & D. Morgan in New Street, above left, catered for ladies and girls who were often served in different shops to men and boys. The photograph was taken in 1921; the building is now demolished. In many ways this was the female equivalent to Tom Grainger's shop (see illustration 18).

16 Cooper Edmonds, above right, was the main local photographer and the man to go to for weddings and other celebrations. Although he did not think much of amateur photographers he would develop and print to a high standard. He had his own studio for portraits which were very artistic in the current style.

17 Like other shops between Bell Street and Duke Street this was once part of the market. The stalls gradually became more permanent until they were turned into shops. There have been many clothiers here but now it is a photography shop. The upstairs windows are wonderfully eccentric with their own gables.

WHERE SHALL I BUY MY
XMAS PRESENTS

Which will be Useful, Sensible, Seasonable, Inexpensive and Acceptable ? *TRY*

T. GRAINGER,

WHO HAS A TREMENDOUS SELECTION OF

HANDKERCHIEFS for Presents—From 3½d. to 3/6.
MUFFLERS for Presents—Silk from 1/11 to 10/6, Cotton from 8½d. to 1/11.
SOCKS for Presents, latest designs, Cashmere, Wool, Silk—9½d. to 4/11.
CAPS for Presents, choice patterns, newest shapes—1/- to 4/6.
TIES for Presents, Knitted, Silk, and Poplin—6½d. to 3/6.
FANCY WOOL JACKETS for Presents, Lemon, Putty, Fawn, Lovat, Heather—6/11 to 25/-.
GENT.'S UMBRELLAS for Presents—A Nice Selection in Silk, Taffeta—7/11 to 30/-.
SILK HANDKERCHIEFS for Presents, lovely colourings—1/- to 4/11
GENT.'S FANCY WOOL VESTS and PULL-OVERS for Presents, neat and choice patterns—10/- to 30/.
MOTOR SCARVES for Presents, Silk Stripes—1/11 to 14/11.
UNDERWEAR for Presents, all leading makes—From 2/11 to 13/6.
GLOVES for Presents, Wool, Suede, Cape, lined and unlined—1/- to 15/6.
SHIRTS for Presents; over 60 doz. to select from in Wool, Union, Print, Cotton—3/11 to 16/6.
KIDDIES' JERSEY SUITS for Presents, Knit Royal make—3/11 to 18/6.
SMALL BOYS' TUNIC SUITS for Presents, American collars—16/11 to 25/-.
BRACES for Presents, elastic or silk, Gent.'s and Boys'—6½d. to 4/6.
COLLARS for Presents, stiff or soft (including Luvisca)—6½d. to 10½d.
HATS for Presents, Hard Felts, Tweed Hats and Velours—5/11 to 14/6.
For Clothing Presents—SUITS, OVERCOATS, TROUSERS, RAINCOATS—Prices to Suit all Pockets.

See Special Xmas Window Display.

Shop Early. Remember an hour to-day is worth three on Xmas Eve.

Be sure of Address—

T. Grainger, Noted Clothier,
New Street, WELLINGTON.

18 Tom Grainger's shop was demolished in the late 1950s, although by then it was Norman Jellyman's. It was one of the few timber-framed buildings left in the town, but unfortunately it became unsafe because the timber was rotten. The prices seen here may seem very cheap but when they are compared to wages then as opposed to now they become more realistic.

19 S. Corbett and Son stood in Church Street between Lloyds Bank and the post office. In the days when horses were a common form of transport, a saddler, especially one as good as Mr. Corbett, was in great demand for the leather trappings for horses and carts. There were several other saddlers and all their shops had a distinctive smell.

20 The fine Italianate façade of the Wesleyan Methodist church in New Street was built by Herbert Isitt in 1883, when many of the merchants and other businessmen of Wellington belonged to the Methodist Church and were able to contribute some of their profits to the building fund. The town and its council were dominated by wealthy, generous Methodists.

21 Mr. Harvey standing in front of his shop in Market Street. He was one of the chief jewellers in Wellington, attracting customers from the neighbouring coalfield towns. The purchase of rings and watches was a sufficiently rare occurrence to warrant a longer journey than groceries. Most jewellers were craftsmen, watchmakers and also opticians.

22 Mr. Harvey was an Urban District councillor, prominent on the Housing Committee. He dealt with slum clearance and rehousing, and Harvey Crescent was named after him. When he retired his two daughters continued to run the shop for many years. The shop front has been altered and there have been other changes, but it is a jeweller's again.

23 The Wellington Gas Co. showrooms in Market Street. The first gasworks in Wellington was built in Tan Bank, for William Edwards, whose portrait used to hang in the Council Chamber but unfortunately has been lost by Wrekin Council. The gasworks was later moved north of Haygate Road, where coal was roasted to produce gas, coke and coal-tar.

24 National elections were very exciting occasions and here we see the declaration of the results outside the Town Hall, above the market in Market Street. This being the 1906 election it can be seen that nearly all the crowd are men, as women were not deemed to be interested in politics and had no vote.

25 Edward Turner of Market Street was mainly a seed merchant. His shop window, under the Town Hall, was filled with a fascinating display of many coloured seeds. His principal customers were the local farmers to whom he delivered, though he also sold pet food over the counter.

26 The Wrekin Mineral Water Works, like the Wrekin Brewery opposite, was owned by O.D. Murphy and Sons. There was a great demand for 'pop' as there still is for cola and other soft drinks. Soon after this picture was taken the works moved to Holyhead Road and the building was taken over by the gas company.

27 This imposingly ornate building was Barclays Bank. For some reason head office decided in the 1960s to demolish it and replace it with a modern utility, in the 'brutalist' style. Since the late 1980s attempts have been made to soften the outlook of the new building to make it more 'user-friendly'.

28 The 'new' All Saints' Church was built in 1790 to replace a much older church, which included some 12th-century glass, after the building was damaged by Parliamentarians during the Civil War. The Lych Gate is a First World War Memorial still used as a focus for Remembrance Sunday services. The churchyard was cleared, grassed over and reconsecrated in 1953-4.

29 Wellington's Roman Catholic Church was erected in 1906 to replace a previous church on Mill Bank, built in 1838. It is dedicated to St Patrick, whose statue can be seen in a niche halfway up the tower. The church stands just to the east of All Saints on the corner of King Street (formerly Back Lane) and Plough Road.

30 The Baptist church in King Street was built by the Particular (or Calvinistic) Baptists in 1807 and enlarged in 1897. In 1920 the Baptists amalgamated with the Congregationalists and built the Union Free church in Constitution Hill. The Baptist church was then taken over by Norah Wellings' world-renowned doll factory.

31 Hiatt's Ladies' College was started by Mrs. Hiatt the wife of a local solicitor. It was situated on the corner of King Street and Albert Road, now demolished, but commemorated by the name Hiatt Avenue. It had an infants' department and Ken Corbett, the agricultural implement manufacturer, claimed to be an old boy at the girls' school.

32 Wellington Public Library, was given the former Guardians' and Parish Offices, Walker Street, by H.H. France-Heyhurst of Overley Hall in 1902 to celebrate the coronation of Edward VII. It later expanded into the Union Workhouse on the right and the cottages on the left. The long list of librarians includes the famous poet, Philip Larkin.

Mrs. Modern says :-

"All done without watching!"

The sure and easy control of heat makes Electric Cooking almost automatic. By the turn of a switch, perfect results are certain. Electric heat never varies. An Electric Cooker keeps all the heat in the right place ... every dish "done to a turn" ... and done to time without watching. Think of the comfort of cooking by electricity in a cool, clean kitchen on a hot summer's day ... and it is so cheap, about one unit of electricity a day per person.

Call at our Showrooms and let us show you how easy it is to have an Electric Cooker installed in your home. Every modern housewife should have a copy of the informative Booklet "Electric Cooking," sent post free on application.

COOK BY ELECTRICITY

WEST MIDLAND JOINT ELECTRICITY AUTHORITY
WALKER STREET, WELLINGTON. Tel. 322.

33 This advertisement was published in 1939, when cooking by electricity was relatively new. The Ironbridge 'A' power station (now demolished) had just begun operations and the Electricity Authority was anxious to increase trade. Their showrooms in Walker Street were very progressive for the time.

34 Both the Bowring Recreation Ground and Wellington Cottage Hospital were given to the town by John Crump Bowring. Here we see the celebrations for the opening of the hospital by Mrs. Bowring after her husband's death. The Cottage Hospital became the property of the NHS, who closed it in 1989, since when efforts have been made to reopen it.

35 J.C. Bowring gave land to 'the people of Wellington' to be used as a recreation ground. The ground lay opposite his house, Bradley Moor, in Haygate Road and because he did not like brass bands he stipulated in the deed of gift that they should not play there. It was extended to the south of Wellington UDC and is now administered by Wrekin Council.

36 Christ Church seen here in 1904, was built as a chapel of ease for All Saints by Thomas Smith of Madeley and is very similar to his church at Ironbridge. Its one bell, dated 1838, is called Great George (nicknamed the gruel bell). Rev. J.P. Abbey, vicar from 1913 to 1962, changed the style of services from evangelical to Anglo-Catholic.

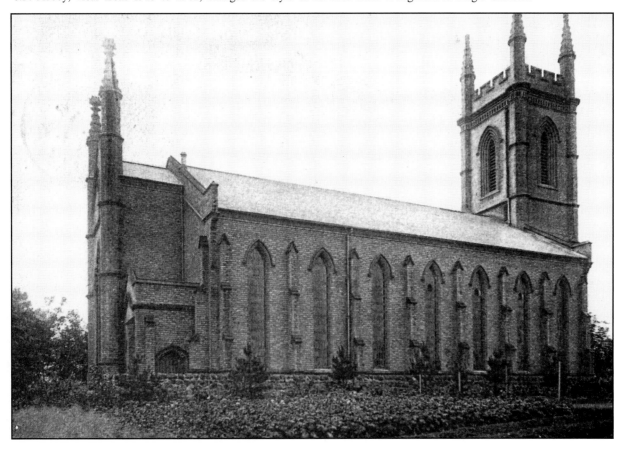

Wellington Town F.C. 1920-21.

37 The *Cock Hotel*, pictured left, is a local landmark. The *Swan* on the right has now been demolished and rebuilt. This was the busiest crossroads in Wellington—it was a notorious A5 bottleneck before the M54 was built. Mill Bank must have had a windmill, one of several in the town.

38 At the rear of the *Bucks Head* inn is the football ground, home of Wellington Town F.C., called the Lillywhites, but now renamed Telford United. The team, below left, is seen in all its glory with the many trophies accumulated during the 1920-21 season. Although quite firmly in England, the Lillywhites won the Welsh Cup three times.

39 Church Street, below, leads from the Green, where a market was held before the 1244 charter, around the churchyard and into the Market Square. At this point it widens and may at one time have been part of a market. On the left was Steventon's the tailors, then Ten Tree Croft, Lloyds Bank, Corbett the saddler and the post office, which later became Agnew's the tailor's.

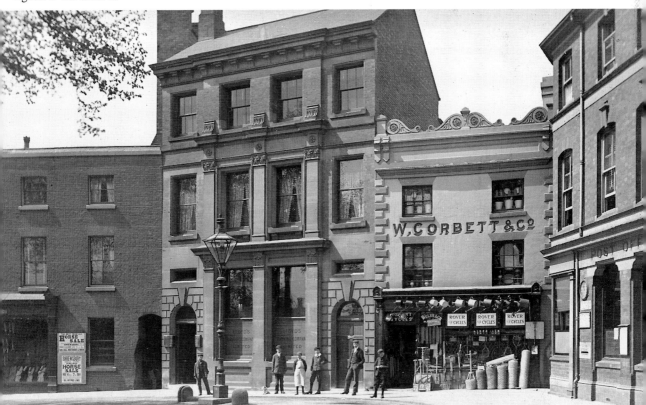

THE OLD HALL

40 The Old Hall in Holyhead Road, formerly Street Lane, is the oldest building in Wellington. It was for many years the home of the Forester family, hereditary foresters of the Wrekin Forest, who gradually acquired more land, from what was the Royal Forest, until they owned most of it. The family moved to Dothill and later to Willey. The Old Hall became a school under Dr. Cranage.

41 Dr. Joseph Edward Cranage founded Old Hall School at 19 years of age. He remained as headmaster for nearly fifty years. He gained an MA and PhD as an external candidate at the University of Jena, having taught himself German. He was a keen local preacher and founded the ecumenical New Hall and Children's Gospel Hall. Ralph Hickman, seen here centre right with his staff and pupils, was headmaster from 1906 to 1926.

42 Until the Second World War Old Hall School kept its own farm, a relic of the Forester days, to feed its boarders. Staff were employed at the farm, often with their wives looking after the boys and school staff, who also 'lived in'. Most of the farmland is now playing fields for the school, which survives.

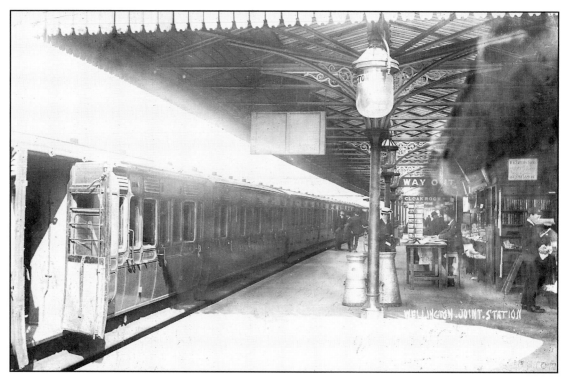

43 Wellington passenger railway station, opened in 1849 and it expanded to be a joint Great Western Railway and London, Midland and Scottish Railway junction of six lines—the main communications centre for east Shropshire. It is seen here in the 1930s with milk churns and Smith's bookshop. The five platforms are now reduced to two and it is a shadow of its former self.

44 Here the Roman Watling Street, later rebuilt by Thomas Telford as the Holyhead Road, is seen looking west. Behind us was the village of Watling Street, later incorporated into Wellington township; ahead the Holyhead Road used to be Street Lane. Both the *Cock Hotel* and the *Swan* (since demolished and rebuilt) were important coaching houses on the London-Holyhead route, later the A5.

45 The 'Double Star' jazz band performed in Wellington and are pictured here between 1936-37. In just over two years most of them were heavily involved in the war and the band did not reform afterwards. They seem very serious young men and rather grand in their uniforms.

46 Wellington Orchestral and Operatic Society was a very lively organisation under their president and prime mover Dr. George Mackie. Their intention was to provide an annual cultural highlight for the town, though some of their ambitious productions took more than a year to rehearse. They used several venues; this picture was taken at the newly built Clifton Cinema in 1939.

THE CLIFTON,   WELLINGTON

Proprietors : CLIFTON CINEMA (WELLINGTON), LTD.
Resident Manager and Licensee : BASIL M. KAY.
'PHONE 430.

Week Commencing, April 24th, 1939

Wellington Orchestral and Operatic Society

(PRESIDENT : DR. GEORGE MACKIE).

PRESENT

Good-Night Vienna

(By Arrangement with Messrs. Samuel French, Ltd).

Evenings at 7-30.

Matinee Saturday at 2-30.

PREVIOUS   PRODUCTIONS:

1927	THE MIKADO	
1928	YEOMEN OF THE GUARD	
1929	THE GONDOLIERS	
1930	IOLANTHE	
1931	MERRIE ENGLAND	

1933	RUDDIGORE
1934	TOM JONES
1935	THE QUAKER GIRL
1937	THE DESERT SONG
1938	MAID OF THE MOUNTAINS

47 George V was crowned King and Emperor in 1911 after the death of his father Edward VII. He was, as we now forget, ruler of the largest empire the world has ever known, with one third of the earth's surface coloured pink on the map to denote that it was 'ours'. In the photograph, above left, a New Zealand flag is being presented in King Street, opposite the Drill Hall. The High Schools were built here, on the site of what is now New College.

48 Coronations were a good excuse for a party, as can be seen in this 1911 view of the Square, below left. It shows a marvellous collection of women's hats, most bought especially for the occasion—no doubt much to the joy of Wellington milliners. Not only people dressed up for the great occasion, the street was also made to look resplendent.

49 Wrekin College, below, then known as Wellington College, was founded in 1880 by Mr. (later Sir) John Bayley, who had previously been headmaster of Constitution Hill Board School. He sold the school in 1920, by which time it had 200 pupils, and had changed its name. Like the Old Hall it continues to prosper.

50 There has always been a strong emphasis on sport at Wrekin College, though some of the extensive playing fields are now being built on. For many years, it was school policy to acquire land and buildings. None of this explains why the 2nd XV has only XIV players in the photograph.

51 Wellington and District Cottage Hospital for many years provided a service for minor injuries and respite care. Local nurses and general practitioners staffed 'The Cottage' until the new Princess Royal General Hospital was built.

52 The Primitive Methodist church in Tan Bank was built in fine red brick, by Elijah Jones in 1898. The Primitives began locally with a meeting on The Wrekin in 1808, gradually separating from the Wesleyan Methodists, though in 1966 the two branches of Methodism amalgamated, leaving the building redundant. It was bought by local Muslims and has since served as Telford Mosque.

53 We have already seen these buildings, the *Cock* and the *Swan*, from the Holyhead Road. We now look from Dawley Road to Mill Bank, where the A5 crossed the A442. Mill Bank must have had a windmill at some time. Wellington also has Mill Lane, and a small rise near Wrekin College was called Windmill Bank. There were windmills from 1315, the last one closing in the latter half of the 19th century.

54 The Ordnance Survey 6": 1 mile map shows Hadley in 1928 as an industrial village with many of the attributes of a small town. In the north is the Castle Car Works of Joseph Sankey and Sons, with the canal running alongside. To the north-east is Trench Ironworks with Blockley's Brick and Tile Works, and off the map to the west is Haybridge Steel. In the centre is the village with church, chapel, public houses and many small shops.

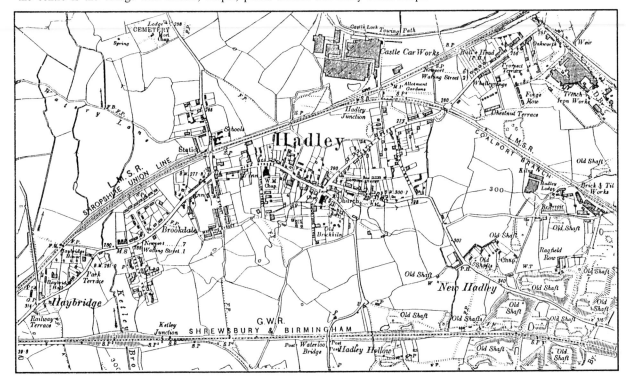

55 Watery Lane, Hadley, is seen here frozen in the snow, though the stream is running freely. Like all the towns and villages now in Telford, Hadley began life as an agricultural settlement and even until recently still had some farmland between the factories and mines. Telford New Town, by taking all available land for development, destroyed the tradition of centuries.

56 Hadley Council School opened as the first purpose-built school in Shropshire in 1874. As the population increased so did the size of the school. Many locals left this school and went on to Oakengates Technical College, either full- or part-time, for most of the jobs in the area demanded technical skills. This is now the Guru Nanak Sikh Temple.

57 Hadley Park windmill is a local landmark, situated near the remains of the canal. It had been converted to a water mill by 1792 and replaced by 1842. It is generally believed that the reason for the name Hadley Castle Works is because this was mistaken for a castle. The mill has been restored and will be preserved.

58 Bricks and tiles have been produced at Hadley since at least 1681. By 1901 B.P. Blockley had opened Ragfield Tileries at New Hadley, and another works, Hadley Tileries, was built nearby in 1912. Blockleys Ltd. added a third works in 1935, advertised here in 1939. By 1963 they were making 20,000,000 bricks a year.

59 This guillotine lock on the Trench branch of the Shropshire Union Canal is another relic from the past. When canals were the principal means of industrial transport this one was vital to the local economy. Difficulties in constructing canals led to the invention of the inclined plane—the first was at Ketley—by which barges were lifted from a low to a high level on a steep rail track.

60 Hadley Park's farmland was gradually swallowed up by development as Hadley expanded, leaving a fine farmhouse but no land. For much of its later life it has been a 'gentleman's residence'. During the Second World War it housed the managing director of Joseph Sankey and Sons, the Canadian Harry Hodgson. It is now a popular hotel.

61 Joseph Sankey and Sons' Hadley Castle Works is seen here in an aerial view of 1918. It has been the largest local employer in the area for many years. Its principle products are anything that can be made from pressed steel, including car wheels, car bodies, car chassis and furniture. Over the years, and even to this day, there have been many defence contracts; Spitfires were assembled here during the Second World War and more recently Warrior armoured vehicles for Bosnia.

62 There has always been, a long tradition of choral music at Hadley, and here is the Hadley Orpheus Male Voice Choir in 1923. The choir has won many honours and continues to do so. For many years the Morgan family have been associated with its leadership, but there are many other local families who have provided members for several generations.

63 Apley Castle was the home of the Charlton-Meyrick family for many centuries. The building dates from 1792-94 and was greatly extended in 1856. The money came from mining royalties on land in the Oakengates, St Georges and Wrockwardine Wood area. The 'castle' was demolished in 1955 and the land was later acquired by the Development Corporation.

64 A view of Apley from across the lake in which one of the Charlton family was drowned whilst trying to ride his horse across. Through the trees on the right lie the remains of an earlier castle, crenellated in 1327. This was damaged in the Civil War, and later by the Development Corporation in an ill-conceived restoration attempt.

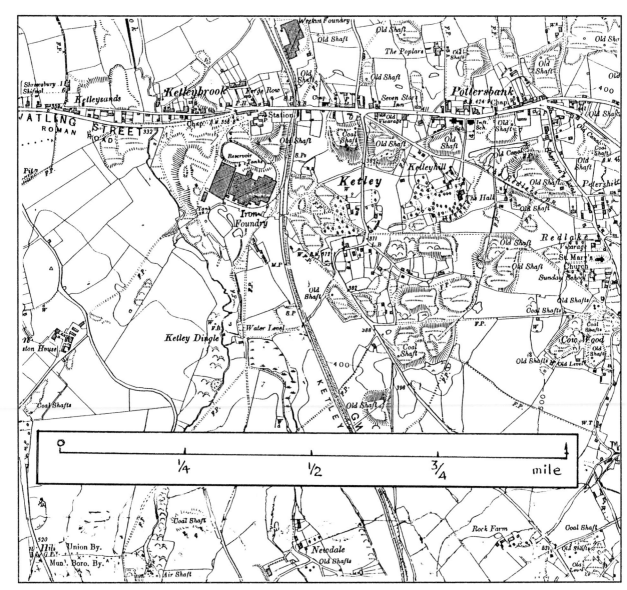

65 The 6": 1 mile Ordnance Survey map of Ketley showing the village in 1928. To the north is the main railway line dividing it from Hadley, with the GWR branch line running north to south; Ketley station is at the point where this crosses Watling Street. The factory to the north, Wrekin Foundry, belonged to James Clay and made agricultural machinery. The larger iron foundry, south of the station was Sinclair's and made rainwater goods such as pipes and gutters.

66 The 'Ketley Dodger', *c.*1900, which often held up traffic on the Holyhead Road was a local institution. The station is on the right of the picture, to the south of the main road. Trains from Ketley to Wellington came into the 'bay'; in the other direction the line went to Coalbrookdale and across the Severn by the Albert Edward Bridge to join the Severn Valley Railway, or across to Much Wenlock.

67 Priorslee Furnaces were a most important part of the Lilleshall Company's empire. Looking at Priorslee now, with its university, ornamental lakes and modern houses it is difficult to imagine it as it was before the Second World War, with its furnaces, pit, rolling mill, steelworks and farm. There are still factories, for example those of Ricoh and N.E.C., but they are very different.

68 John Maddock & Co. of Oakengates was one of the few large ironworks in the area not directly controlled by the Lilleshall Company or the Coalbrookdale Company. They began by making nails and small iron parts for boots and developed into specialists in a great variety of small castings. The works finally closed in August 1987.

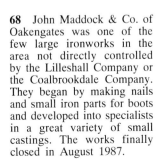

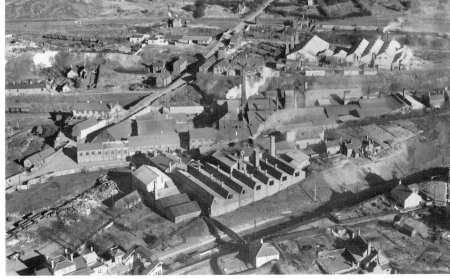

69 Oakengates town band in 1930. It was considered one of the best brass bands in the area and performed frequently for the public. Perhaps it had something to do with the fact that Oakengates has long been associated with the Salvation Army's centre in what is now Telford, and that it has the largest theatre in the area.

70   The Molineux butchers' Christmas show on 13 December, 1913. All the prize animals had been bought at Wellington Smithfield and slaughtered at the back of the shop in Market Street. Seen here from left are: J. Bailey, C. Duckett, Mrs. Dallow, George Shepperd, (delivery boy, then 12 years old) and Mr. Dallow. What a wonderful antidote to war!

71 Corfield's grocery and provision merchants, above left, in 1918. The staff included: Mr. William Corfield, G. Ward, Miss M. Price, Jessie Corfield, Miss Samson, Mr. W.R. Corfield (the owner), G. Burdett, H. Corfield, E. Smout and H. Burdett. The firm competed with the Oakengates Co-op but was considered more up-market. Oliver's next door, was a branch of their Wellington business.

72 The old ambulance, photographed here, was originally a bus obtained from Mr. William Owen of Oakengates in the early 1930s. The group of people in the picture helped provide this much needed service and included: T. Pearce, H. Powell, Mr. Holland, Mr. Nock, H. Evans, N. Brown, W. Corfield, S. Bolas, C. Ferriday, T. Poppit, T. Price, Dr. Kennedy, T. Hayward, A. Holl and Mr. Perkins.

73 In 1938 a new ambulance was purchased and a dedication service was held by the bishop of Stafford. In the picture are: B. Dabbs, T. Hayward, T. Owen, W. Corfield, T. Price, A. Holl, T. Hopley, Lord Bradford, Dr. Kennedy, Rev. G. Cartlidge (who wrote a local history), Rev. N.S. Kidson and H. Hilton. The ambulance was the product of much effort and generosity.

74 Oakengates Wakes, seen here in 1905, were held annually in Owens Fields, which are now under the road to Donnington. Until the end of the last century bull-baiting and cock-fighting were a regular feature of the Wakes, and this was the last place in Shropshire where these events were held. By 1900 they had become a funfair as shown here.

75 Bridge Street and the corner of Hadley Road. On the left, behind the iron gates, is the recreation ground, usually known as 'the Rec'. In 1927 the miners' welfare fund organised the levelling of a pit mound at the bottom of Hartshill, and eventually its facilities included a bowling-green, tennis courts and a football pitch.

76 Snedshill Brickworks in 1940 was owned by the Lilleshall Company, the most important employer in Oakengates. The works produced literally millions of bricks from local clay, enabling the company to prosper in the building trade. Later they diversified into sanitary ware. In the foreground are stacks of pig-iron from Priorslee Furnaces, which also belonged to the company. The chimneys were local landmarks until their demolition.

77 Oakengates Scout troop, seen here in 1919, was clearly a keen collection of lads. Their musical instruments are on display, a feature of some troops at the time, though later the practice of Scout bands was discontinued in many cases. There were, and still are, troops of Scouts and Guides in most of the local towns and villages, Wellington at one time having four.

78 A view of Oakengates, left, taken from the top of Albion Pit Bank in 1928, before it was planted. In the foreground, behind the advertising hoarding, the top of a beehive-shaped watch-box, can be seen, as well as the remains of a disused canal and a small field adjoining a cottage occupied by Mr. Jones and his daughter. Owens Field is the open ground to the left, beyond which is a large house belonging to Mr. Meese, the dentist.

79 A loaded cart stands in front of Corfield's warehouse, below left, with Mr. Ward, the driver. The photograph was taken in 1920, when cars and vans were few and far between and most deliveries were by horse and cart. The grocery trade was far more labour intensive than it is now, providing more service and delivering goods free if orders were of more than £1 in value (£4 was considered a good weekly wage).

80 The picture below shows a typical view of market day in 1925. The Green was cut in half by the railway. The hill on the other side of the bridge is Charlton pit mound which was later removed by voluntary labour and cleared to make the recreation ground. The market started early and continued until it was dark, when crowds gathered to buy leftovers at reduced prices.

81 The Grosvenor Cinema was built in the early 1920s. Casual labour was employed to prepare the site but the men had to bring their own shovels. Mr. Whitefoot, the ironmonger and hardware dealer, gladly supplied these and accepted payment by instalments. There was a great deal of 'tick' or credit dealing during hard times.

82 Oakengates had its Holyhead Road as did Ketley and Wellington, the same Roman Watling Street rebuilt by Thomas Telford to connect London and Dublin by stagecoach and ferry. Here it is in 1905, looking towards Snedshill, the site of one of the Lilleshall Company's large complexes.

83 Miss Jenks, Mrs. Barratt and Miss Gladys Onions were the three teachers of the old Wombridge school who transferred to the Hartshill school; they are pictured a the school entrance. At the time this building was thought to be very advanced.

84 Opposite the Snedshill Brickworks was Snedshill Forge, also owned by the Lilleshall Company. A great deal of employment in Oakengates and for many miles around depended on the fortunes of the Lilleshall Company. Fortunately the company had many irons in many fires: bricks, iron-founding, coal and iron mining, engine manufacture, chemicals, coke, coal-tar and so on, so there was usually work to be had.

85 This view of Oakengates shows it as a smoky, grimy town surrounded by pit mounds, as indeed it was, yet more smoke meant more work, which was often in short supply. What it does not show is the skilful, friendly, cheerful and reliable people who lived here.

86 The Oakengates rail tunnel begins just east of the station; the main Shrewsbury to Birmingham line occupies an increasingly deep cutting leading into a tunnel. Here is the west entrance. Above the tunnel was a crossroads, where the main road to Shifnal met Station Road and the route to Ketley Bank.

87 The east end of the tunnel. In addition to the roads mentioned above there were five railway lines, including the Coalport line, mineral lines and work sidings. There was also the old canal. All these routes met within the short space of a few hundred yards. Most of the land around was mined at various times so there were also mine-workings under the tunnel.

88 Oxford Street is at right angles to Market Street on the south side. The *Royal Exchange* is advertised as a commercial hotel, meaning it wished to attract commercial travellers who toured the area taking orders for their firm's products.

89 The Perfection Series was a postcard company's trademark, not a comment on the beauty of the views they depicted. Actually many of these pit mounds possessed great beauty in the wildflowers they attracted. One comment made concerning the recent 'tidying up' of the mounds was that the view looked better before the flowers were bulldozed.

90 The building on the right was the Oakengates Coffee Palace—a rather incongruous name for an area which had a reputation for bull-baiting, cock-fighting and drunkenness. It was because of this that the local inhabitants who wished to change its public image tried to encourage the drinking of coffee instead of beer. Regrettably it was demolished by the Telford Development Corporation.

91 Oakengates Park (or Recreation Ground), above left, is an excellent example of what can be done for land restoration with local goodwill and hard work. In 1927 the miners' welfare fund was responsible for levelling a pit mound on which a public recreation ground was opened. A bowling-green, football pitch and tennis courts were among the facilities provided.

92 The Wombridge Church of St Mary and St Leonard, below left, was built in 1757 on the ruins of the lady chapel of St Leonard's Priory which had been in use since the Reformation. The Augustinian Priory of St Leonard at Wombridge was one of the main centres of the royal forest of Mount Gilbert (The Wrekin), though there are few traces left.

93 Holy Trinity Church, above, was built in 1854 and immediately given its own parish, carved out of the parishes of Wombridge and Shifnal. Two years later a vicarage was built on land given by St John Chiverton Charlton of Apley Castle, who was deriving a considerable income from mining royalties on his family's land in the parish.

94 John Maddock & Co. Ltd., above left, began producing nails in Stirchley around 1869. The company moved to Oakengates in 1878, and expanded into toe protectors, bicycle parts, cylinder blocks and a variety of malleable iron products. Employment varied greatly: 200 in 1891, 575 in 1960 and 86 in 1983. The works is now demolished.

95 Primitive Methodism came to Shropshire when W. Saunders preached at Ketley Bank and Wrockwardine Wood in 1821, and James Bonsor preached in Oakengates Bull Ring to 2,000 in 1822. The Wrockwardine Wood Methodist church, below left, was built in 1823, despite the opposition of the vicar of Wombridge to the siting of a nonconformist chapel in his parish.

96 St Georges Reading Room and Institute, below, began in 1875 and in 1899 this fine building was erected on a site given by the 4th Duke of Sutherland. It seems to have always been used for a combination of education and social functions, including billiards. The county library have made good use of the building, as have such organisations as the Good Neighbours old people's club.

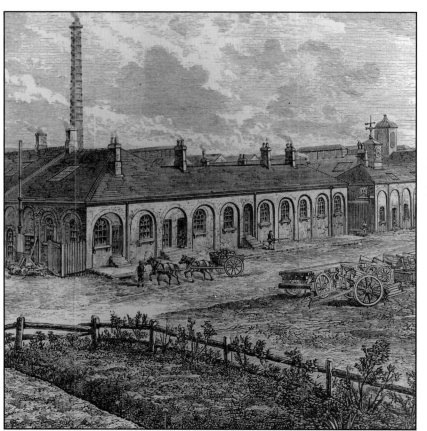

97 The Lilleshall Company's Great Foundry and Engine Factory was part of the company's comprehensive empire. Having mined the coal, iron and limestone, produced pig-iron in its furnaces, and refined its products, the company began to make finished goods such as steam engines. Some of these were used to pump water from their own pits, blow air into their furnaces and pull their own railway trucks.

98 St Georges Methodist church is in Church Street, on the south side of the road. The Rev. R.C. Cameron, who was perpetual curate of Wombridge from 1808 to 1856, vigorously opposed all nonconformists, though the population was growing much more rapidly than the Church of England could cope with. His influence, however, resulted in chapels being built outside his parish.

99 The first Church of St George was built in Pains Lane as a chapel of ease in 1806, changing the settlement's name, though this was not officially confirmed until 1915. The land was provided by the Marquess of Stafford and building costs were met by the Lilleshall Company. This church replaced it in 1862, the tower with its carillon being added in 1929.

100 This boot scraper at St Georges is a good example of the small castings produced at Maddock's foundry in Oakengates. These articles were essential for every home when most of the roads were transformed into a sea of mud at the slightest hint of rain. Even main roads were poor by modern standards, while side streets and lanes had little or no hard surface.

101 There was a strong temperance movement in the area, which took many forms, one of which was St Georges Temperance Band, seen here in 1905. The boy sitting in the front was to distinguish himself as a musician; he is William Shuker, who became conductor of the St Georges Orchestra.

102 William Shuker, the boy in the previous photograph, is here being presented with a collection of classical records by Sir John and Lady Barbirolli in recognition of his 50 years' service conducting the St Georges and District Orchestra. The picture was taken at the Civic Hall, Wolverhampton by the *Shropshire Star*.

103 Market Street, Oakengates, was the town's main shopping street. It had developed from the Roman road, where there had been a market, and was lined with shops as the railway brought prosperity to the town. Along here came parades on Wakes Days. We are looking west towards the Coffee Palace and the railway bridge with its motto, 'The brightest little town in Salop'.

104 The Wrekin Brewery, owned by O.D. Murphy and his sons, prospered in spite of the temperance movement. The ales, beer and mineral waters were produced in Wellington but consumed all round The Wrekin. They were so popular that the firm was able to buy up most of the local pubs and hotels as there was little competition. Eventually all were sold to Greenall Whitley.

105 The gardens, lake and summerhouse of Priorslee Hall. For many years this prestigious house was the headquarters of the Lilleshall Company and the residence of its senior local manager. The company, though owned by landed aristocrats, owes its considerable success to the skills and integrity of its managers and agents.

106 The library of Priorslee Hall illustrates well the very civilised style of living enjoyed by its occupants. The house was acquired by Telford Development Corporation who used it as offices, building many sheds at the back for its increasing staff. It is now the nucleus of the University in Shropshire, a campus of the University of Wolverhampton.

107 Priorslee Furnaces belonged to the Lilleshall Company. Until 1879 all iron had been cast or wrought, but in that year Thomas and Gilchrist invented the basic Bessemer process, suitable for local ores. This steelworks was built in 1882 under the direction of Gilchrist. Air was blown through furnaces in the pear-shaped converters.

108 This coal distillation plant was part of the Priorslee Furnaces complex. The German company Distillation AG erected coke ovens and a by-products and benzole plant, Shropshire's only 20th-century integrated coke ovens and by-products plant to use chamber type ovens instead of the open heaps of circular ovens which had served the industry since Abraham Darby I.

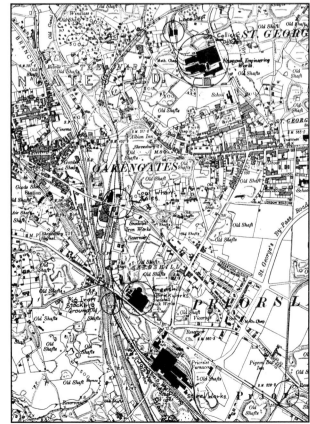

109 The 6": 1 mile Ordnance Survey map of 1928 has been added to by the Lilleshall Company to show their holdings. The large factories and relatively small settlements are contrasted. When marvelling at the intricacies of the Snedshill junction it must be remembered that it rests upon a network of mines.

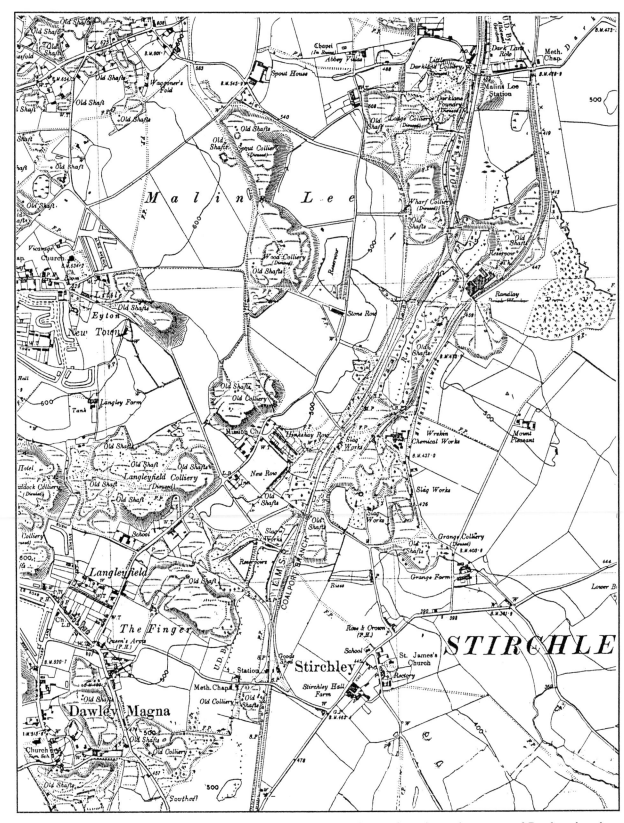

110 The 1928 Ordnance Survey shows Dawley Magna to be some distance from the modern centre of Dawley; there has often been confusion about where Dawley becomes Little Dawley, for what we now think of as the town centre was Dawley Market. There is a large number of mine-shafts and mounds shown, but it is interesting to see how many fields there were.

111 High Street, Dawley, was the main road from Wellington to Bridgnorth when this photograph was taken in the 1920s, and for many years after. Shopping became increasingly difficult as the volume of traffic on this route grew. The large building on the right is the market hall; the weekly market is now in the pedestrianised street.

112 The Finger, or Finger Road as it is now officially called, shows that the older houses were more individualistic than their modern counterparts. An older name for this road is Peter's Finger. In the middle of the picture is the *Queen's Head Inn*, often now called the *Queen's Finger*.

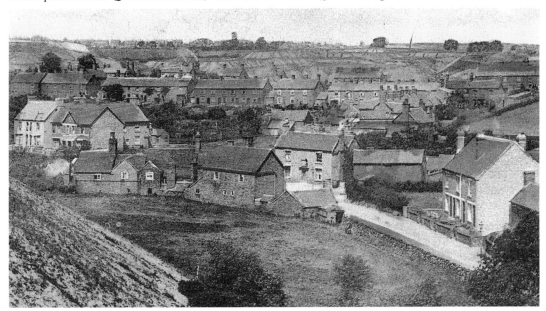

113 There is a story (said to have originated in Wellington) that when Captain Matthew Webb returned in triumph after becoming the first man to swim the English Channel, a Dawley man put his pig on the wall to see the band go by. Pictures were staged by various press photographers and this is one of them. Capt. Webb died in 1883 attempting the Niagara rapids and whirlpool.

114 St Leonard's Church at Malinslee (built in 1805) is very similar to Telford's Madeley church and must have been influenced by the latter's design. Its exterior plan is an elongated octagon though inside the chancel is oblong, with triangular sacristies. The big square tower is on the west side and the windows are in two tiers.

115 Malinslee railway station is typical of the many small stations scattered around the coalfield towns and villages. Sometimes when a station was built there would be a growth of houses and shops around it, in some cases the station came before the settlement. A station was within walking distance of almost everywhere until motor traffic took over.

116 The 12th-century chapel in Malinslee was a ruin long before Telford was designated. It has since been painstakingly reconstructed on a strong concrete raft in the Town Park as a tourist feature; a better fate than Dawley Castle whose ruins are beneath a pit mound.

117 & 118 The lights and fountain monument to Matthew Webb at the crossroads of High Street and New Street, seen below and on the opposite page. It was moved from here to Paddock Mound to make way for traffic, but local pressure insisted on its return and it is now back where it should be. 'Nothing great is easy' was Webb's motto; he was born in a house which used to stand near the monument.

Memorial Fountain, Dawley

Nothing great is easy. Erected by public subscription to the memory of Captain Matthew Webb, who, in addition to feats of life saving, swam the English Channel. Captain Webb was born at Dawley, January 19, 1848, and lost his life in an attempt to swim Niagara Rapids on July 24, 1883. He was born in a house which formerly occupied a site a few yards from this memorial.

119 St Luke's Church at Doseley seen here in the snow. Because Dawley is higher than most of the area there is an expression 'Dawley weather' for any unpleasant conditions. Designed by R. Griffiths of Broseley, St Luke's was built in 1845 of red and pale grey brick and sandstone dressings. It has a timber south porch, and a western bell turret with one bell.

120 A school board was formed compulsorily at Dawley in 1875. Langley School, opened in 1878 and pictured here, was their first school. There had been few private schools in the area. The standard of elementary education at Pool Hill and Langley schools was said by the inspectors to be high towards the end of the 19th century.

121 The area around the Dark Lane settlement is now the site of Telford's shopping malls. It is seen here as mainly an agricultural area, though some of the land is rough grazing. The railway line is still used for carrying coal to Buildwas power station from the West Midlands.

122 The close-packed rows of Dark Lane were inhabited until their occupants were moved and the houses demolished to make room for new development. Some of the people resented being moved and still dream of returning. The close-knit community was destroyed.

123 This view of Horsehay Pool shows the beginning of a long row of cottages built for local workers. It is a well-built row, facing the pool. Apart from mining and the Horsehay Works there was work at the basalt quarry, the pipe-works, the potteries, on the canals and railways, and local farms.

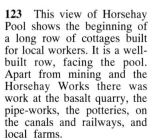

124 Station Road connects Horsehay and Dawley. Most of the little communities in what is now Telford had their own railway station until after the Second World War. Rail was important for industry too, and most freight was carried in this way, with every works having its own sidings, shunting engines and trucks. Most were heavy industries needing a lot of bulk transport.

125 Horsehay Works changed with the times; it was bought in 1886 by the Simpson brothers of Rotherham and concentrated on building bridges, roofs and girders, employing 500 men by 1900. The 'Sentinel' steam waggon was developed here, and later a gas plant was constructed. After the Second World War heavy cranes, including the travelling variety, bridges and mining equipment were produced.

126 Horsehay's famous Round House was, as is clear in the photograph, a house constructed within an old bottle kiln. It was a well-known landmark, as was Cinder Hill. Much of the slag generated from iron-working was later used for road-building and for glass manufacture; there are also many lumps of furnace slag in older rockeries.

127 The Horsehay Works, seen here, was perhaps most famous for its bridges, which were exported to many parts of the world. They were fine bridges and many of them still stand as a monument to British engineering, supporting roads and railways over great rivers. Locally the problem was moving the huge sections on enormously long loaders which disrupted traffic.

128 Horsehay, whether under the Simpson brothers, the Horsehay Company Ltd., Adamson Alliance or Adamson-Butterley Ltd., was constantly undergoing restructuring, rebuilding or reorganisation. This was partly due to the sheer size of many of its products. Bridges and cranes were often 'one-off' and needed a different shaped space from the last.

129 Madeley is an ancient settlement, although most houses in the parish now are less than thirty years old. Here are some of the timber-framed cottages in Queen Street seen from the back, where their age is better appreciated. They are good examples of pre-industrial domestic architecture.

130 Park Street, Madeley, is seen here just before the Second World War, when it was a small, quiet town in the rural borough of Wenlock. There were mines, industries and a shopping centre which provided a sufficient range of services for the inhabitants. Now the town is sandwiched between huge high-density housing estates and modern industrial complexes.

131 St Michael's Church is an interesting example of a church built not by an architect but by the engineer Thomas Telford, in 1796. It is octagonal in shape but the inside of the nave is oblong, with a narrower chancel, the vestries cutting off two triangles. It is said to have been built on a pre-Christian mound.

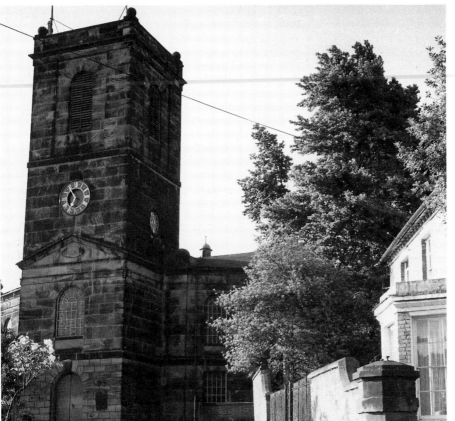

132 St Michael's tower is on the west side of the church. It is a square building with an arched entrance and arched window over, then a pediment with free-standing square upper stages. In the church-yard are several cast-iron tombs, notably one to Rev. John Fletcher, a Swiss who was friend and biographer to John Wesley and, with his wife, most influential in the revivalist movement.

133 The Madeley Wesleyan Methodist church was built in Court Street in 1841-2 to replace a more modest one built in 1833. John Wesley first came to Madeley in 1764, and many times subsequently. John Fletcher and later his wife Mary, preached to Methodists who were still members of the Church of England and still attended communion. Their adopted daughter, Mary Tooth, continued after their death.

134 The Anstice Memorial Institute and Workmen's Club, above left, is said to have been the first of its kind, and opened in 1869. The building is Italianate in style and contained a reading room, library and large lecture hall. It has been altered many times over the years to accommodate plays, social occasions and especially dances. It was very well restored by the Development Corporation.

135 The older part of Madeley is seen here, below left, from the top of St Michael's Church tower. We are looking north up Church Street towards the town centre, with Anstice Hall standing proud above the shops and market. The old vicarage is a fine building, as is Madeley Hall and its barns.

136 The picture below shows the workmen's cottages at the Coke Hearth, Lightmoor. There is also a place called Coke Hearth at Coalbrookdale. Until the mid-19th century coke was produced for the furnaces in the same way it had been for Darby in 1709, by heating coal in large heaps; the gas and tar were wasted.

137 Jiggers Bank is the road that leads down the upper part of the valley of the Loamhole Brook. Coal, iron and limestone were brought down here for the furnaces at Coalbrookdale in the 19th century when this picture was taken. In the 1920s a car which did not have to change down into bottom gear up this hill was a good one!

138 Here is the Loamhole (or Lumhole) Dingle seen from Jiggers Bank, looking west towards the Rope Walk. The houses are on Darby Road, near the Quaker burial ground. Just down the valley is the furnace belonging to the Brooke family of Madeley Court where Abraham Darby I produced iron using coke to fire his furnace. The site is preserved and is the key to the whole Ironbridge Gorge Museum.

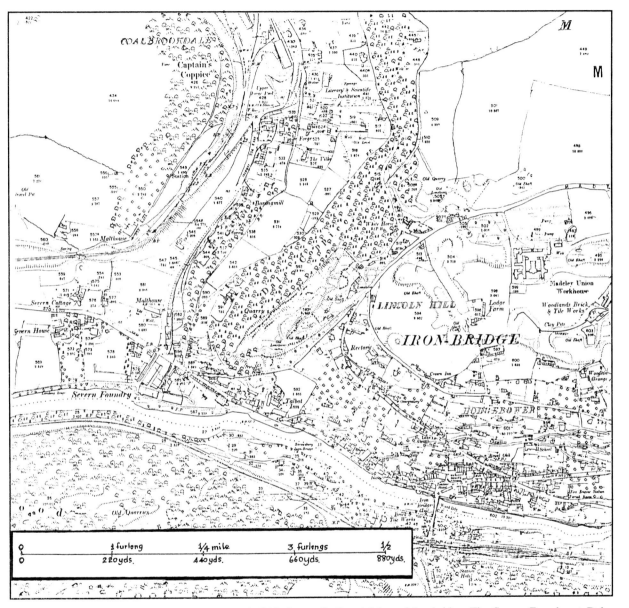

139 The 25": 1 mile Ordnance Survey map of 1902 shows Coalbrookdale and Ironbridge. The Severn Foundry at Dale End is now divided between a toy and teddy bear factory, and an antiques centre. The closely-built settlement of Ironbridge is seen to be clinging to the south-facing side of the steep gorge with its diagonal roads and footways. It shows ferries operating across the river.

140 The view of Coalbrookdale from the south shows the works on the left; it had gradually crept down the valley from the first furnace. In the centre is Holy Trinity Church and below it the Coalbrookdale Institute, built for educational and cultural activities, then used as an art school and now as a Youth Hostel.

141 The Loamhole or Lumhole brook has this waterfall high up its valley. The stream, then called the Caldebrook (which gave Coalbrookdale its name) was the principal reason for the siting of a furnace. Even before Abraham Darby I's time water-power was needed to blow air into the furnace. Several reservoirs were constructed in the valley to keep the water-supply regular.

142 Holy Trinity Church was built with money given by Abraham Darby III, who had forsaken his family's Quaker origins and joined the Church of England; his tomb is on the east side. Although perched on a very steep hillside the building has remained stable since 1854.

143 Coalbrookdale from Benthall Edge and the view, taken with a long lens, is similar to that from the south (illustration 140) but has the passenger station on the left. Although the passengers are long gone the station is now used by the Green Wood Trust, and the line carries coal to the electricity power station.

144 The Rotunda, seen here around 1900, was an important source of limestone which was the essential flux when ironstone was being heated to extract the iron. 'Sunday walks' were constructed on the hill. The Severn Warehouse in the foreground has also been a mineral water factory and is now part of the museum.

145 Twenty or thirty years later trees have grown over part of the Rotunda. This hill is of Wenlock limestone and is honeycombed with mine-tunnels. There are occasional landslips throughout the gorge, which is geologically recent (less than 10,000 years) and unstable.

146 Except when this picture was taken, Coalbrookdale station was very busy in the late 19th and early 20th centuries. Just up the line from here is a tall viaduct from which hang stalactites, created by rain dissolving the trucks' cargoes of lime, which would then drip down onto the track.

147 Rose Cottage was said to be an early farmhouse; it is certainly dated 1642 and has been altered and enlarged several times. It is next to the stream which rushes down the dale, and may have been the residence of a works' manager. It has been very carefully restored. There is an old forge just up the road.

148 Coalbrookdale County High School, formerly the secondary school, was opened in 1911 for 75 boys and 75 girls, but initially only 46 boys and 24 girls attended. It attracted pupils from as far away as Cound and Presthope. Originally conceived as two separate schools it merged in 1932, and in 1965 amalgamated with Madeley Modern at Hilltop to become Abraham Darby comprehensive. It is now a primary school.

149 Ironbridge at the turn of the century; here the bridge is much flatter than it is now. It had always been assumed that cast iron would never bend, but a glance at the bridge from this position now shows that the 375 tons of iron have bent quite considerably, presumably due to the immense pressure on each side. The buildings on the left of the bridge have long since disappeared.

150 An engraving of Ironbridge, *c.*1850. The houses and shops leading up to the bridge have long been demolished. The large building by the bridge is the *Tontine Hotel*. Steps lead up to St Luke's Church and there are far fewer houses in Church Hill. On the skyline is Hodge Bower.

151 The Wharfage, photographed from the south side of the bridge, near where the toll-house was sited. The water is low at this time and it would have been difficult to load the barges and trows (large shallow-draft river craft) which were such a feature of the river. Lincoln Hill and The Rotunda are in the background.

152 In 1900, at the height of a terrible flood, the Severn River had risen about three metres over the Wharfage. There is now less variation in the water-level as the reservoirs at Clywedog control the amount of water in the Severn. There are records of the river freezing over and people skating on it.

153 Ironbridge seen here from the south in the 1920s. Bridge tolls were charged for pedestrians as well as vehicles. The bridge was closed to traffic in 1934, and the proprietors conveyed it to the county council in 1950. The difficulties of building in such a steep valley are well illustrated.

154 Ironbridge railway station, *c*.1907, above left, is built on the Jackfield or south side of the river as part of the Severn Valley Railway. For passengers wishing to go to Wellington one would first have to travel to Buildwas Junction and then change trains. The line has long gone and the site is now a car park, though past Bridgnorth the SVR is preserved.

155 St Luke's Church, Ironbridge, below left, was built in 1836 with financial help from the Madeley Wood Company, and accommodated 1,062 people. Although built on the cheap by a local firm (Thomas Smith of Madeley), and on an extremely difficult site, it is now admired for its excellent acoustics.

156 The Great Western Railway opened the Albert Edward Bridge, below, in 1864 to link Wellington and Much Wenlock, though much of its traffic brought Wenlock limestone to the foundries. Last used for passengers during a temporary revival in 1979, it continues to supply coal to Buildwas power station.

157 The ferry plied its trade between Benthall Edge and Ironbridge, just downstream of the Albert Edward railway bridge. The north side of the river bank was prone to flooding, though this has been filled with fly-ash from the first electricity power station, and has for many years been the site of boathouses for the local rowing club.

158 The passage-boat from Jackfield operated as an important ferry which enabled workers to cross the river without taking a long detour via the iron bridge. It was attached to a cable across the river, using the water-pressure on the rudder as power, like the ferry at Hampton Loade. After the First World War it was replaced by the Jackfield footbridge.

159 Down the steep valley from Broseley to the Severn came a swift stream which powered this huge wheel which in turn worked the corn mill. It is 'under-overshot', that is to say the water reaches the wheel by the high trough, falls into 'buckets' on the rim and forces the wheel backwards. The famous Laxey wheel on the Isle of Man operates similarly.

160 The Coalport and Jackfield Memorial Bridge is seen in this unique picture of its ceremonial opening. The crowds on each bank are joining in to celebrate the end of the war with relief, and pleasure that they had something much more useful than the average war memorial, though perhaps the ferry operators were not so pleased.

161 The Church of St Mary at Jackfield was built in 1863 by Blomfield. It is an unusual shape, with an odd octagonal turret in the angle between the nave and the chancel, which has short columns at the bell stage and a conical roof. It is in pale and strong red, yellow and blue bricks with geometrical tracery in its windows. It makes a delightful silhouette.

162 Tommy Rogers of Ironbridge. The Rogers family have been making and using traditional coracles, like this one, for many generations—perhaps for over a thousand years! Until quite recently they had a reputation (earned or not) for illegal poaching. Now, however, Eustace Rogers is rightly respected internationally as a true craftsman.

163 The Free (or Haynes Memorial) Bridge was built in 1909 of prestressed ferro-concrete to connect Coalport and Jackfield, saving a journey via either of the iron bridges. It was well-used but became unsafe and, in spite of attempts to have it preserved, was finally demolished and replaced in 1994.

164 The incline is now a tourist attraction. The rails carried wheeled trolleys supporting the barges. The bottom canal, running just above the Severn, led to the Coalport China Works, which used coal from the higher land above. Just to the right is the tar tunnel, built for access to a coal mine, which exuded coal tar and made great profit for its owners.

165 Coalport China Works in the early 19th century. From 1796 to 1875 John Rose, the founder, and his family made a great range of richly-decorated, flower-encrusted porcelains here, with plain teaware and tablewares. In the 19th and early 20th centuries about four hundred workers were employed and Coalport china was collected by almost every local family, usually being kept for 'best'.

166 This old bottle kiln, seen here in 1968, saw long service in firing china at Coalport. Many artists were employed designing and decorating the work; other workers burnt bones to mix with the clay, or worked as potters, sagger-makers and so on. The works closed in 1926, after a strike in 1923 in difficult trading times, and moved to the Potteries. This place is now a working museum.

167 A wooden bridge was built on this site in 1780, called Preen's Eddy, and is commemorated by the *Woodbridge* public house on the south side. This Coalport bridge was built in 1799 as a three-rib structure by John Onions and John Guest, but two ribs were added, and the abutments improved 20 years later after a fracture in the middle rib.

168 The ironworks in the Blists (or Blesses or Blisses) Hill area is now a major part of the Ironbridge Gorge Museum, housing many buildings which have been transported there from other places. When this photograph was taken, early this century, the works was in full operation. The Madeley Wood Company moved furnaces here in 1832, 1840 and 1844, for it was a site by the canal and near their mines.

169 The Wrekin is seen here from the top of the Ercall with Lawrence Hill between, looking south-west along The Wrekin fault. Between the Ercall and Lawrence Hill there are now huge quarries from which millions of tons of Wrekin Quartzite have been taken for the foundations of Telford. The track along the ridge is wide and leads through Hell and Heaven Gates into the ancient hillfort of the Cornovii.

170 Seen here from the south-west The Wrekin looks conical, though in fact it has a 'hog's back' shape. The nearer hill is the Little Hill, formerly called Primrose Hill. On the skyline is the Needle's Eye, through which all 'true Salopians' have climbed. The fair, once held on the top, was discontinued because of drunken fights.

171 The water-supply, up until the middle of the 19th century, had been taken from wells, but around 1850 reservoirs were constructed. In 1905 a large new reservoir at the Forest Glen tapped a stream and began to supply the Wellington area; from 1920 onwards this was supplemented by artesian wells, like the one here, bored into the triassic sandstone aquifer to the north.

172 Taken from near Hell's Gate, the lower of two entrances to the hillfort, this photograph looks north-east along the main fault line. It is the opposite view from the one shown in illustration 169. The town seen over the Ercall's shoulder to the left is Wellington. Hadley, Ketley, Donnington and Oakengates are also in the picture.

173 The Forest Glen Pavilion was built in 1898 by Henry Pointon to refresh the many visitors to The Wrekin. It belonged to the Pointon family, including 'Ossy' and 'Percy' for nearly a century, and became a venue for dinners and dances, hosting 'all friends round The Wrekin'. It was recently moved to Blist's Hill Museum.

174 The Wrekin Cottage (Halfway House or Upper Cottage) was a great feature of regular pilgrimages to The Wrekin, serving ham and eggs, teas and mineral waters. Orders were taken on the way up and when the walkers returned meal and appetite coincided. Children were amused by 'swingleboats' (swingboats), ponies and goats. It is now a private house.

175 The Needle's Eye is a rock formation on The Wrekin which forms a narrow cleft. It has many traditions, especially that all true Salopians must climb through the crevice, from west to east; young girls must not look back or they will never marry. It was almost certainly a religious symbol in Celtic times. Although disturbed in a recent earthquake it can still be climbed.

Bibliography

Although some of the information in this book has come from the memories, researches and friends of the authors, who have lived in the area for many years, much of it has come from the admirable books which are listed below. We are most grateful to their writers, in particular, G.C. Baugh, D.C. Cox, A.J.L. Winchester, P.A. Stamper and J. McFall of the *Victoria County History*. The following books are recommended reading; those out of print are in Wellington Local Studies Library.

Baugh, G.C. (ed.), *A History of Shropshire*, vol. XI, Telford, *Victoria County History*, Oxford U.P., 1985.

Blackwall, A., *Historic Bridges of Shropshire*, Shropshire CC, 1985.

Brierley, D.J. (*et al.*), *Shropshire County Guide*, Shropshire CC, several, undated.

De Soissons, M., *Telford, The Making of Shropshire's New Town*, Swan Hill, 1991.

Evans, G., *Wellington, A Portrait*, S. B. Publications, 1990; *Lost Villages of Telford*, S. B. Publications, 1991; *Telford's Living Landscape*, Vision Books, 1993; *Shropshire's Wonderful Markets*, Vision Books, 1994; *Secrets of The Wrekin Forest*, Vision Books, 1992.

Foreman, H., *The Old Dissent*, Union Free Church, 1986.

Frost, A.J., *Priorslee Remembered*, Frost, A.J., 1993.

Gale, W.K.V. and Nicholls, C., *The Lilleshall Company*, Moorland, 1979.

Garner, L., *Churches of Shropshire*, Shropshire Books, 1994.

Gilder, T., *Hadley at War*, Gildertext, 1992.

Glover, G., *Shropshire Eccentrics*, Arch, 1991.

Lenton, J.H., *Methodism in Wellington*, Methodist Church, 1982.

McCrea, M., *A History of The Parish Church of All Saints*, All Saints, Wellington, 1987.

Morris, J. (ed.), *Domesday Book, Shropshire*, Phillimore, 1986.

Morriss, R.K., *Canals of Shropshire*, Shropshire Books, 1991.

Oppitz, L., *Shropshire & Staffordshire Railways*, Countryside Books, 1993.

Otter, L., *Wellington, A Town with a Past*, Civic Society, 1990.

Pevsner, N., *The Buildings of England, Shropshire*, Penguin, 1958.

Peet, G. (ed.), *The Dawley Book*, Wrekin Council, recent; *The Madeley Book*, Wrekin Council, 1991; *The Ironbridge Book*, Wrekin Council, 1991.

Raven, M.A., *Shropshire Gazetteer*, Raven, M.A., 1989.

Smith, A. (*et al.*), *Memories of Old Wellington*, vols. 1, 2, 3 and 4, Wellington Civic Society, 1991.

Stanford, S., *The Archaeology of the Welsh Marches*, Stanford, 1980.

Toghill, P., *Geology in Shropshire*, Swan Hill, 1990.

Trinder, B., *The Darbys of Coalbrookdale*, Phillimore, 1974; *A History of Shropshire*, Phillimore, 1983; *The Industrial Revolution in Shropshire*, Phillimore, 1973; *Ironbridge & Coalbrookdale*, Phillimore, 1988; *Yeomen & Colliers in Telford*, Phillimore, 1980.

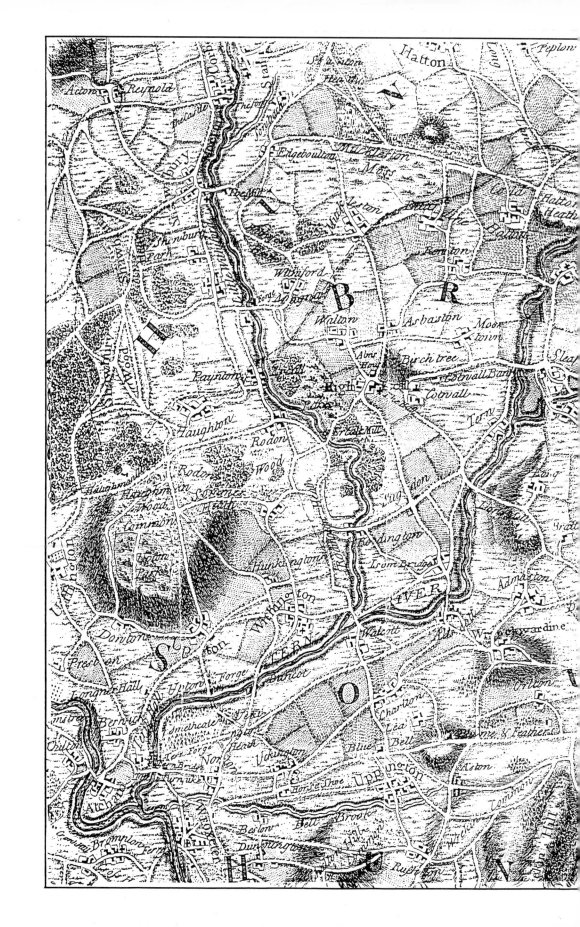